WINDOWS ON THE WORLD

WHALES
DOLPHINS,
AND PORPOISES

Written by
Mark Carwardine

Illustrated by
Martin Camm

DORLING KINDERSLEY
London • New York • Moscow • Sydney

DK

A Dorling Kindersley Book

Editor Miranda Smith
Art editor Sheilagh Noble
Designers Peter Radcliffe,
Christopher Gillingwater

Senior art editor Chris Scollen
Managing art editor Jacquie Gulliver
Managing editor Ann Kramer

Editorial consultant Dr Peter Evans
Production Shelagh Gibson

Published in Great Britain by
Dorling Kindersley Limited,
9 Henrietta Street, London WC2E 8PS

Paperback edition
2 4 6 8 10 9 7 5 3 1

Copyright © 1992, 1998 Dorling Kindersley
Limited, London
Text copyright © 1992 Mark Carwardine

Visit us on the World Wide Web at:
http://www.dk.com

A CIP catalogue record for this book is available
from the British Library.

ISBN: 0-7513-5734-0

Reproduced in Singapore by Colourscan
Printed and bound in Spain by Artes Gráficas Toledo, S.A.
D.L. TO: 41-1998

CONTENTS

WHAT IS A WHALE?

Whales look rather like fish, but they are more closely related to people. Like us, they are mammals; in other words, they are warm blooded, breathe air and give birth to babies instead of laying eggs. The main difference is that we live on land and they live in the water. Whales are so perfectly adapted to an aquatic life that they have lost their back legs, their front legs have turned into flippers and they almost never come ashore.

There are many kinds of whale, and 78 species have been identified so far. These include all the animals in a group which scientists call the "cetaceans", but which most people call simply whales, dolphins and porpoises. They come in a variety of shapes and colours, and they all have different habits and lifestyles. In size alone, they range from a tiny dolphin just over 1m (3ft) long, to the blue whale, which stretches to more than 30m (98ft).

Is it a whale or a fish?

At first sight, a whale really does look like a fish - especially a fish as large as this whale shark. The two creatures have remarkably similar body shapes and they both have fins, flippers and huge tails. In fact the similarities are so striking that, for many years, whales were thought to be fish. But take a closer look and you will see many important differences.

Fatty!

Unlike most other mammals, whales do not have thick coats of hair to keep them warm - these would slow them down while they were swimming. They have a layer of blubber, or fat, instead. The blubber of whales living in very cold water can be as much as 50cm (20in) thick.

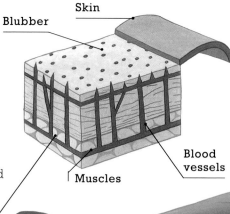

Skin

Blubber

Blood vessels

Muscles

The whale's tail swings up and down

Telling tails

It is easy to tell which of these two animals is a whale and which is a fish - just by their tails. The whale's rubbery tail, called a fluke, is horizontal. The shark's tail, called a caudal fin, is vertical. They are both used for swimming.

The shark's tail swings from side to side

A whale's skin is silky smooth to touch, but a shark is covered in thousands of rough, tooth-like scales

The whale shark has three "extra" fins which are not found on whales, dolphins or porpoises

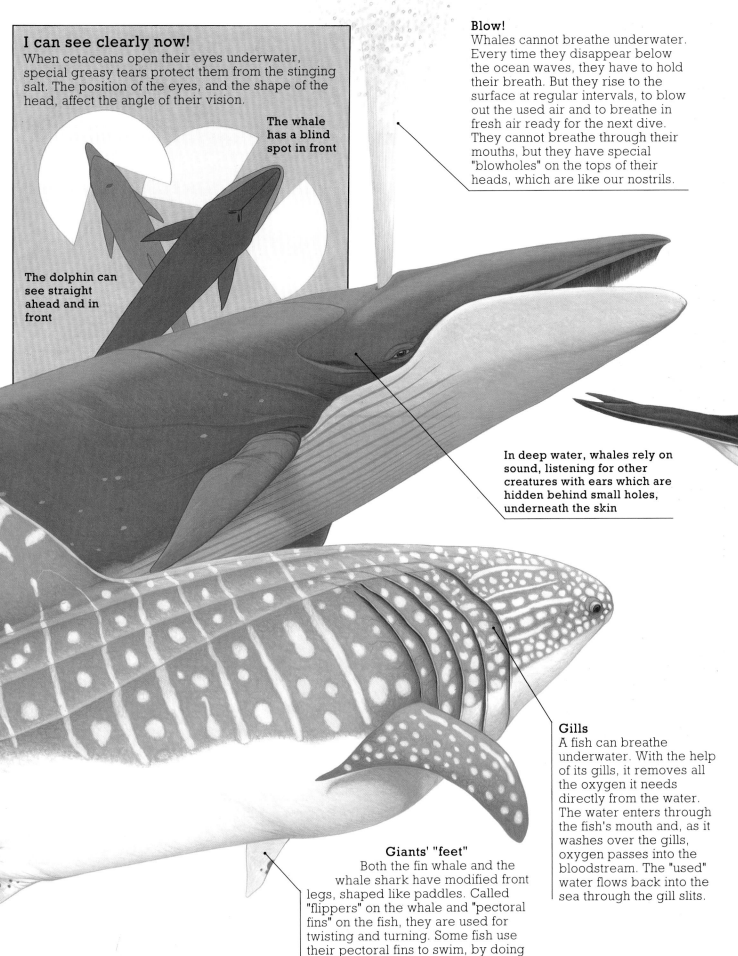

I can see clearly now!

When cetaceans open their eyes underwater, special greasy tears protect them from the stinging salt. The position of the eyes, and the shape of the head, affect the angle of their vision.

The whale has a blind spot in front

The dolphin can see straight ahead and in front

Blow!

Whales cannot breathe underwater. Every time they disappear below the ocean waves, they have to hold their breath. But they rise to the surface at regular intervals, to blow out the used air and to breathe in fresh air ready for the next dive. They cannot breathe through their mouths, but they have special "blowholes" on the tops of their heads, which are like our nostrils.

In deep water, whales rely on sound, listening for other creatures with ears which are hidden behind small holes, underneath the skin

Gills

A fish can breathe underwater. With the help of its gills, it removes all the oxygen it needs directly from the water. The water enters through the fish's mouth and, as it washes over the gills, oxygen passes into the bloodstream. The "used" water flows back into the sea through the gill slits.

Giants' "feet"

Both the fin whale and the whale shark have modified front legs, shaped like paddles. Called "flippers" on the whale and "pectoral fins" on the fish, they are used for twisting and turning. Some fish use their pectoral fins to swim, by doing a kind of doggy-paddle.

5

What's in a name?

The main difference between whales, dolphins and porpoises is their size. But there is so much variation within each group that the distinction is not as simple as it sounds. Some whales are smaller than the largest dolphins, and some dolphins are smaller than the largest porpoises. With so much overlap, it is not surprising that even the experts are sometimes rather vague about the differences between each group. To add to the confusion, most species are known by many different names, in many different languages.

Is it a whale or a dolphin?

Basically, whales are the "big ones", usually longer than 4m (13ft) and dolphins are the "little ones". But there are many exceptions and even their names can cause confusion. Many so-called "whales" are really dolphins - the melon-headed whale, the southern right whale dolphin and the long-finned pilot whale among them.

The pygmy right whale never grows longer than 6.4m (21ft)

This killer whale is having a snooze; whales do not sleep like we do, but they doze on the surface of the sea, or nod off for a few moments while they are swimming

The killer whale is a dolphin, although it can grow to nearly 10m (33ft) long

Home sweet home

Whales, dolphins and porpoises live in warm waters at the equator, in the freezing cold waters around the poles, in muddy rivers hundreds of kilometres inland, or even at great depths far out to sea.

Rivers and estuaries

Several dolphins and porpoises spend all or part of their lives in fresh water. Amazon river dolphins are found exclusively in the flooded forests of the Amazon and Orinoco river systems.

Coastal waters

The Heaviside's dolphin, which lives off south-west Africa, is never seen far out to sea. Like many members of the family, it prefers to stay in coastal waters, where it feeds on squid and bottom-dwelling fish.

The black dolphin is only 1.2m (3ft 11in) long and much smaller than most porpoises

Dall's porpoises reach a length of 2.2m (7ft 3in), and are stockily built

1 Fin whale
2 Whale shark
3 Killer whale
4 Pygmy right whale
5 Dall's porpoise
6 Black dolphin

Is it a dolphin or a porpoise?

In the United States, every small cetacean is generally referred to as a porpoise. But in other parts of the world, this name is used only for the very smallest. Strictly speaking, though, there are only six porpoises (pages 42-43) - and they all belong to the same family. They have small triangular fins (or none at all) and reduced beaks.

How a dolphin swims

A dolphin swims with the help of powerful muscles in the rear third of its body. With smooth, measured movements, it sweeps its horizontal tail up and down, making the flukes work like a ship's propeller to drive it through the water.

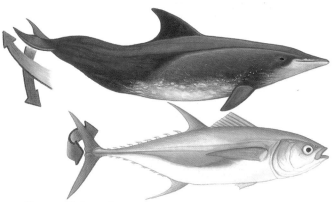

How a fish swims

A fish swims by wriggling its body like a snake. It moves its head from side to side, sending "waves" down its body. The waves grow bigger until they reach the tail, which then swings from side to side.

Open sea

Northern bottlenose whales are deep divers and rarely live in water less than 200m (656ft) deep. Atlantic white-sided dolphins also enjoy living in the open sea, often many kilometres from the nearest land.

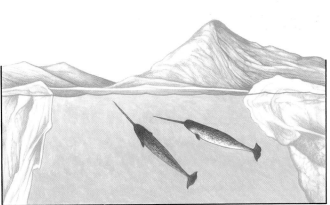

Polar waters

Several whales and dolphins live in icy conditions. Narwhals live in the freezing waters of the high Arctic and have been recorded very close to the North Pole. They are rarely found far from loose pack ice.

KEEPING TRACK

For many years, the only information we had about whales, dolphins and porpoises came from dead animals washed ashore, or the ones killed by whalers and fishermen. People studied a number of live dolphins in captivity, but it was a long time before scientists began to learn about the really wild creatures lurking in the ocean depths. In fact, we have probably discovered more about them in the last 20 years than ever before.

Killer whales off the west coast of Canada, southern right whales in Argentina and the famous bottlenose dolphins of western Australia are just some of the populations which have now been studied in considerable detail. Some amazing techniques have been developed to gather new information. Special depth-recorders can be attached to their fins to measure how deep they dive, waterproof microphones record all their gossiping underwater and, most exciting of all, their movements can even be tracked by satellite.

Who are you?

Sometimes it is possible to recognize individual whales and dolphins by their scars and other markings. This is important because it helps scientists to learn more about their daily lives. They can study a single animal to find out how often it breathes, how far it travels, who it lives with and, finally, when it dies. The scientists are like detectives, piecing together its life story.

Name badges

Some species are almost impossible to tell apart by their natural markings. They all seem to look alike, so they have to be given special name badges, or tags. Many different tags have been used over the years, such as the spaghetti and plate tags on two of these short-snouted spinner dolphins. The third has numbers branded on its fin.

Plate tag

Spaghetti tag

Where are you?

The scientists in this boat cannot see the dusky dolphins in the water below - but they know they are there. They have dropped a waterproof microphone, called a hydrophone, down into the water. With this device, they are listening for the tell-tale sounds of the dolphins chattering to one another.

Dusky dolphins are very inquisitive and bold

What are you doing?

Some tags can be seen from a long distance away, so scientists can watch the particular dolphins they are studying through binoculars. However, other tags provide useful information only after the animals are dead.

Branded numbers

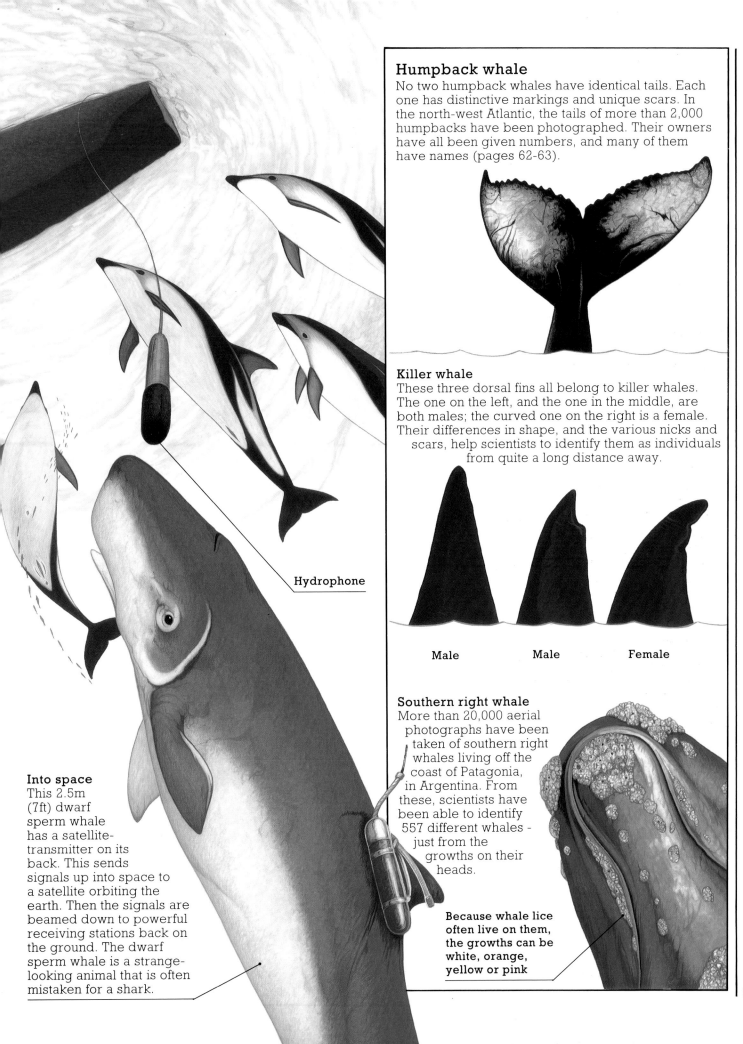

Humpback whale

No two humpback whales have identical tails. Each one has distinctive markings and unique scars. In the north-west Atlantic, the tails of more than 2,000 humpbacks have been photographed. Their owners have all been given numbers, and many of them have names (pages 62-63).

Killer whale

These three dorsal fins all belong to killer whales. The one on the left, and the one in the middle, are both males; the curved one on the right is a female. Their differences in shape, and the various nicks and scars, help scientists to identify them as individuals from quite a long distance away.

Male   **Male**   **Female**

Southern right whale

More than 20,000 aerial photographs have been taken of southern right whales living off the coast of Patagonia, in Argentina. From these, scientists have been able to identify 557 different whales - just from the growths on their heads.

Because whale lice often live on them, the growths can be white, orange, yellow or pink

Hydrophone

Into space

This 2.5m (7ft) dwarf sperm whale has a satellite-transmitter on its back. This sends signals up into space to a satellite orbiting the earth. Then the signals are beamed down to powerful receiving stations back on the ground. The dwarf sperm whale is a strange-looking animal that is often mistaken for a shark.

INSIDE AND OUT

Millions of years ago, a strange wolf-like animal used to hunt for fish at the water's edge. Covered in fur, and with small hooves instead of claws, it sometimes tried swimming doggy-paddle. As the years passed, it spent more and more time in the water, and less on land.

No-one knows for sure, but it may have been an early ancestor of modern whales and dolphins.

There are many clues which suggest that they evolved from furry land animals with four legs. Their skeletons, in particular, are a very important source of information and, at the same time, reveal many of the special adaptations for their life underwater. For example, their front legs have been modified into simple paddles, and apart from a little clump of useless bones floating in the muscle, their back legs have been lost altogether during the course of evolution.

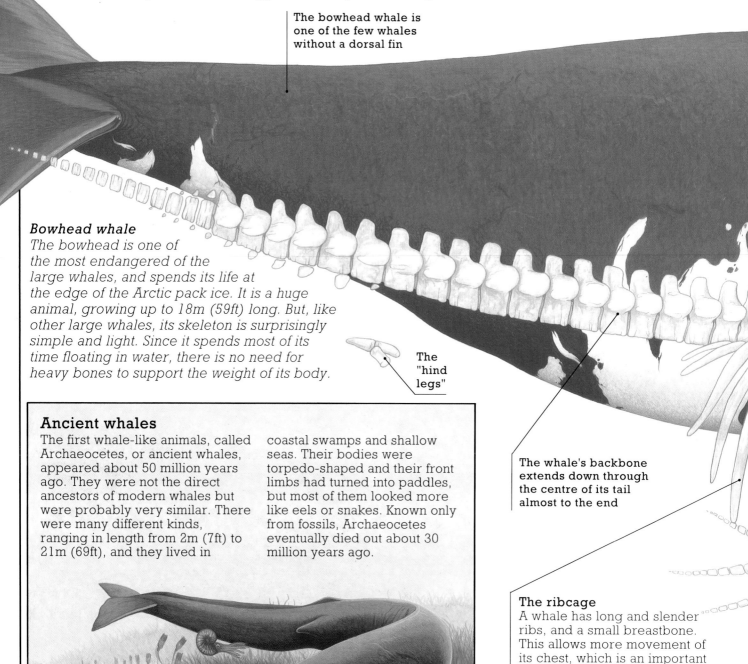

The bowhead whale is one of the few whales without a dorsal fin

Bowhead whale
The bowhead is one of the most endangered of the large whales, and spends its life at the edge of the Arctic pack ice. It is a huge animal, growing up to 18m (59ft) long. But, like other large whales, its skeleton is surprisingly simple and light. Since it spends most of its time floating in water, there is no need for heavy bones to support the weight of its body.

The "hind legs"

The whale's backbone extends down through the centre of its tail almost to the end

Ancient whales
The first whale-like animals, called Archaeocetes, or ancient whales, appeared about 50 million years ago. They were not the direct ancestors of modern whales but were probably very similar. There were many different kinds, ranging in length from 2m (7ft) to 21m (69ft), and they lived in coastal swamps and shallow seas. Their bodies were torpedo-shaped and their front limbs had turned into paddles, but most of them looked more like eels or snakes. Known only from fossils, Archaeocetes eventually died out about 30 million years ago.

The ribcage
A whale has long and slender ribs, and a small breastbone. This allows more movement of its chest, which is an important adaptation for deep diving. But it means that, when the whale is stranded (pages 54-55) and is lying on a beach out of water, the ribs are not strong enough to support the weight of its body, and the animal usually dies.

10

The skull

The skulls of modern whales vary greatly from species to species. The sperm whale has one of the strangest because it is designed to hold the animal's enormous "nose". Its lower jaw is also unmistakable, armed with two neat rows of strong teeth. The bottlenose whale has a similar skull, although all but two of its teeth are tiny and virtually useless. The gently curving grey whale's skull, by contrast, has no teeth at all.

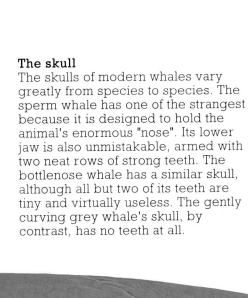

Sperm whale

Grey whale

Bottlenose whale

The characteristic white patch under the chin of the bowhead helps to identify this rare species

The jaw

The name "bowhead" comes from the animal's upper jaw, which is arch-shaped and designed specially to hold the long baleen plates. The plates are considerably longer than in any other whale and may grow up to 4m (13ft) in length. Like most whales, the bowhead has a rather grotesque skull.

The bowhead's skull is one third of the length of its body

The neck

Giraffes, chimpanzees, whales and all other mammals have seven bones called vertebrae, in their necks. Some, or all, of these are usually joined together in the necks of cetaceans. As a result, most members of the family have short, stiff necks which are essential for swimming at high speed. Without them, their heads would wobble and the bones would break.

11

DOWN IN ONE

Whales, dolphins and porpoises eat many different kinds of food. Their choice depends on whether or not they have teeth. Most of the larger whales have no teeth at all, and they feed on shoaling fish or tiny, shrimp-like creatures called krill (page 63). The whales have hundreds of furry, comb-like strands hanging down from their upper jaws. These are called "baleen plates" or "whalebones".

To chew or not to chew?

Most whales, dolphins and porpoises do not need to chew their food; they swallow everything whole. Sperm whales are the most amazing swallowers. The stomach of one sperm whale contained 28,000 tiny undigested squid; others have swallowed a man's boot, a large rock, an old bucket and other strange objects, by mistake.

The plates overlap, with their stiff hairs forming a sieve to filter the food out of the seawater. The whale takes in many tonnes of water in a gulp and, with its baleen plates, can filter out all the fish or krill in a matter of seconds. Dolphins, porpoises and other whales with teeth have to work harder to catch their food. Most of them eat fish or squid, which they chase and grab one at a time.

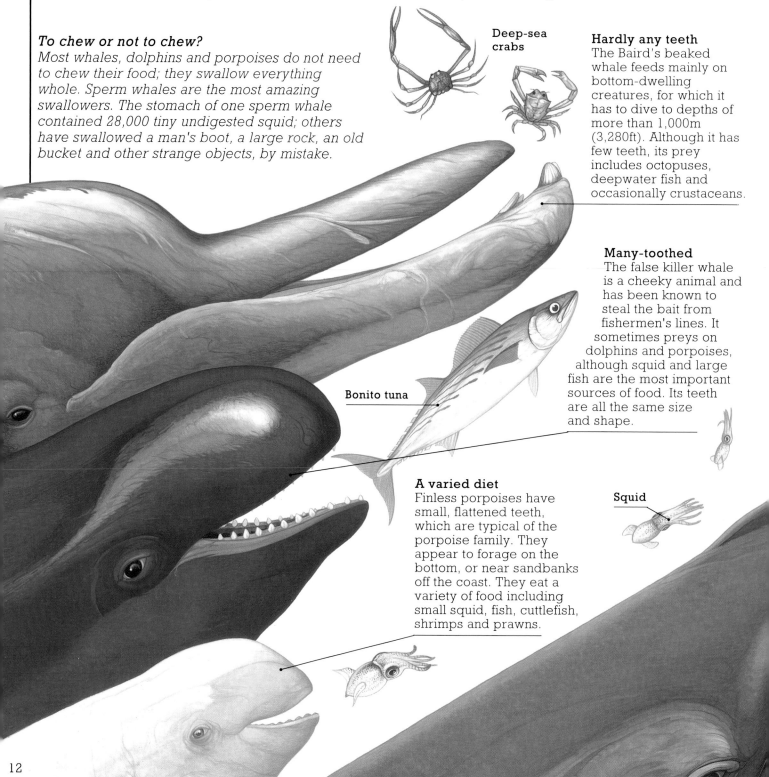

Deep-sea crabs

Hardly any teeth
The Baird's beaked whale feeds mainly on bottom-dwelling creatures, for which it has to dive to depths of more than 1,000m (3,280ft). Although it has few teeth, its prey includes octopuses, deepwater fish and occasionally crustaceans.

Many-toothed
The false killer whale is a cheeky animal and has been known to steal the bait from fishermen's lines. It sometimes preys on dolphins and porpoises, although squid and large fish are the most important sources of food. Its teeth are all the same size and shape.

Bonito tuna

A varied diet
Finless porpoises have small, flattened teeth, which are typical of the porpoise family. They appear to forage on the bottom, or near sandbanks off the coast. They eat a variety of food including small squid, fish, cuttlefish, shrimps and prawns.

Squid

Filtering food

This sei whale is skim-feeding. It swims along with its mouth slightly open and takes in huge quantities of seawater. In a good feeding area, the water will be teeming with fish or tiny shrimp-like animals, called krill (page 63), which are swept into the whale's mouth. The water itself flows straight through and out again, but all the animals are trapped inside by the baleen plates. Every so often, when the whale is ready to swallow, it wipes them off with its tongue, which resembles an enormous jelly-filled cushion.

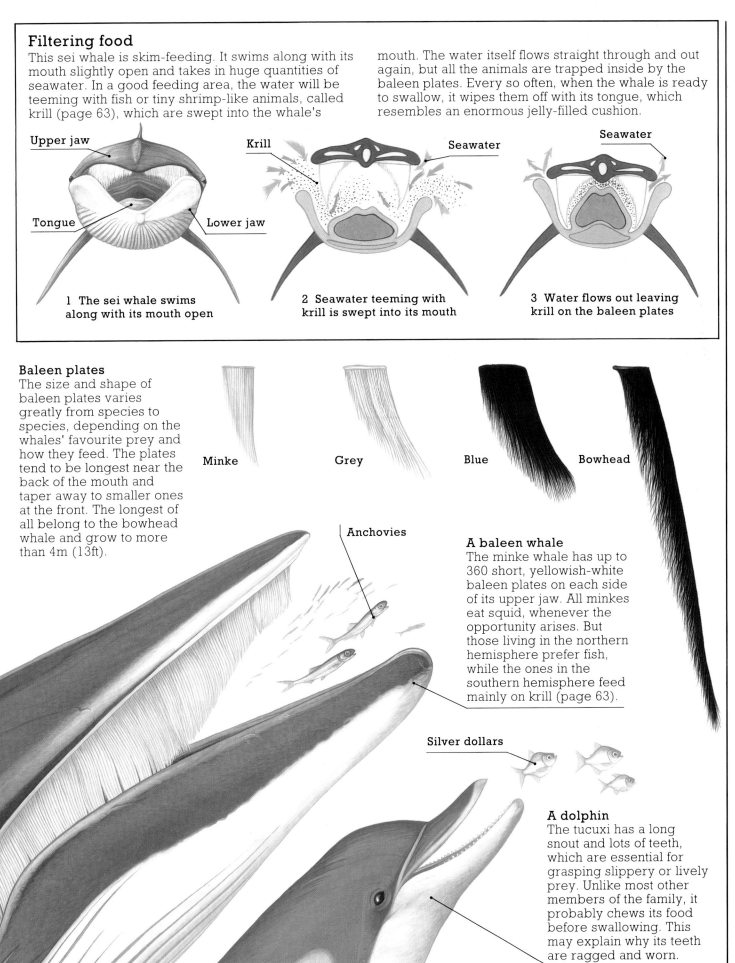

Upper jaw

Tongue

Lower jaw

1 The sei whale swims along with its mouth open

Krill

Seawater

2 Seawater teeming with krill is swept into its mouth

Seawater

3 Water flows out leaving krill on the baleen plates

Baleen plates

The size and shape of baleen plates varies greatly from species to species, depending on the whales' favourite prey and how they feed. The plates tend to be longest near the back of the mouth and taper away to smaller ones at the front. The longest of all belong to the bowhead whale and grow to more than 4m (13ft).

Minke

Grey

Blue

Bowhead

Anchovies

A baleen whale

The minke whale has up to 360 short, yellowish-white baleen plates on each side of its upper jaw. All minkes eat squid, whenever the opportunity arises. But those living in the northern hemisphere prefer fish, while the ones in the southern hemisphere feed mainly on krill (page 63).

Silver dollars

A dolphin

The tucuxi has a long snout and lots of teeth, which are essential for grasping slippery or lively prey. Unlike most other members of the family, it probably chews its food before swallowing. This may explain why its teeth are ragged and worn.

THE FEEDING GROUND

Finding food can be a problem for whales. They need a lot to eat, yet their favourite meals are often available only in certain parts of the world at specific times of the year. Whales are always on the lookout for new areas, but they have been visiting the best feeding grounds for many centuries. The richest pickings tend to be in the cold waters of the extreme north or south, especially during the summer. Antarctica, Cape Cod, Newfoundland, Alaska and several other places attract large numbers of whales to their rich feeding grounds. The gentle giants spend several months at these "whale restaurants", eating as many fish and krill (page 63) as they can. There is very little to eat at their breeding grounds nearer the equator so, by the end of the summer, they have put on enough weight to be able to live mainly off their fat reserves for the rest of the year.

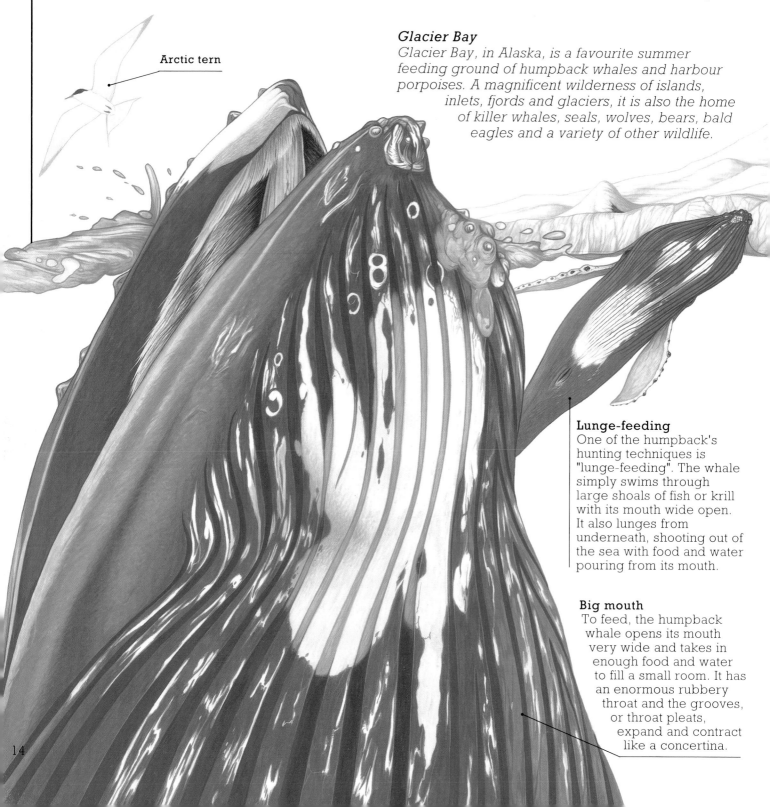

Arctic tern

Glacier Bay

Glacier Bay, in Alaska, is a favourite summer feeding ground of humpback whales and harbour porpoises. A magnificent wilderness of islands, inlets, fjords and glaciers, it is also the home of killer whales, seals, wolves, bears, bald eagles and a variety of other wildlife.

Lunge-feeding

One of the humpback's hunting techniques is "lunge-feeding". The whale simply swims through large shoals of fish or krill with its mouth wide open. It also lunges from underneath, shooting out of the sea with food and water pouring from its mouth.

Big mouth

To feed, the humpback whale opens its mouth very wide and takes in enough food and water to fill a small room. It has an enormous rubbery throat and the grooves, or throat pleats, expand and contract like a concertina.

14

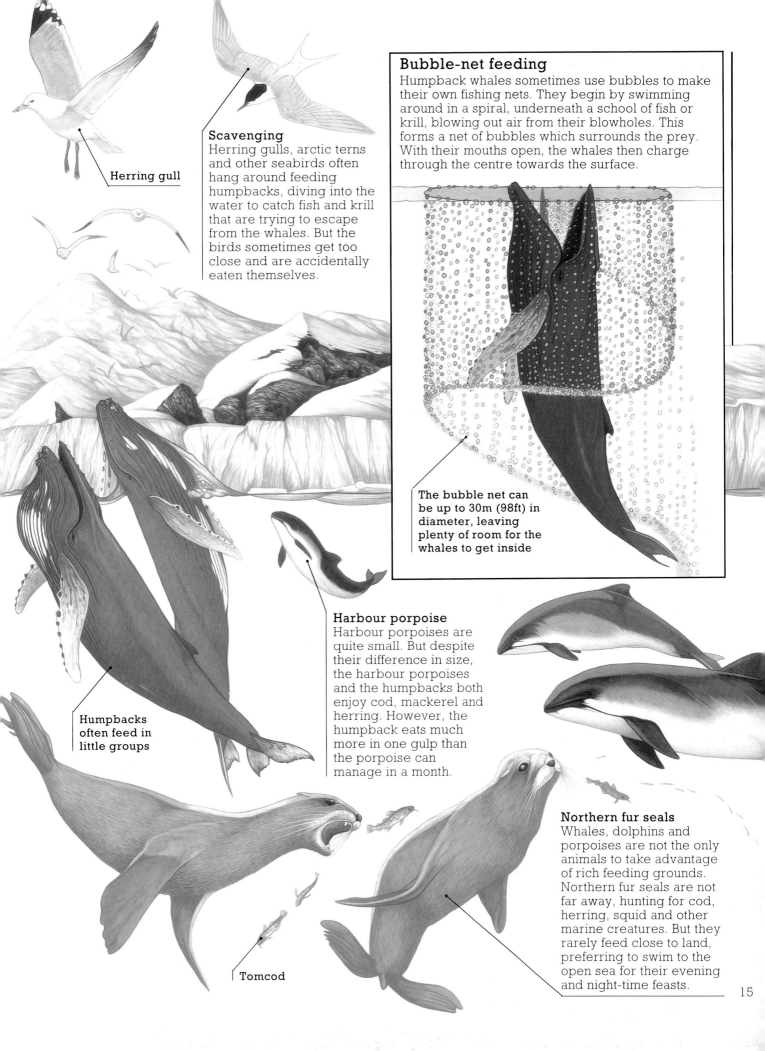

Herring gull

Scavenging
Herring gulls, arctic terns and other seabirds often hang around feeding humpbacks, diving into the water to catch fish and krill that are trying to escape from the whales. But the birds sometimes get too close and are accidentally eaten themselves.

Bubble-net feeding
Humpback whales sometimes use bubbles to make their own fishing nets. They begin by swimming around in a spiral, underneath a school of fish or krill, blowing out air from their blowholes. This forms a net of bubbles which surrounds the prey. With their mouths open, the whales then charge through the centre towards the surface.

The bubble net can be up to 30m (98ft) in diameter, leaving plenty of room for the whales to get inside

Humpbacks often feed in little groups

Harbour porpoise
Harbour porpoises are quite small. But despite their difference in size, the harbour porpoises and the humpbacks both enjoy cod, mackerel and herring. However, the humpback eats much more in one gulp than the porpoise can manage in a month.

Tomcod

Northern fur seals
Whales, dolphins and porpoises are not the only animals to take advantage of rich feeding grounds. Northern fur seals are not far away, hunting for cod, herring, squid and other marine creatures. But they rarely feed close to land, preferring to swim to the open sea for their evening and night-time feasts.

HARMLESS KILLERS

Killer whales have a fearsome reputation as powerful and efficient hunters. They have strong jaws armed with rows of long, sturdy teeth, designed to grab and tear apart other animals. Secure in the knowledge that they have no natural enemies of their own, they roam the seas tackling prey as large as blue whales. But killer whales do not deserve their "killer" name. They never hunt for fun and so are no different from other meat-eaters, most of which have to kill in order to survive. Unlike other top predators, such as lions, tigers and polar bears, killer whales never hunt people, and there has only been one "attack" in the wild. This was on a surfer, who survived after the whale realized its mistake and spat him out. Many people have swum with killer whales and lived to tell the tale.

The killer whale's name
The name "killer whale" probably comes from a phrase which was used by Spanish whalers in the 18th century. They called them "killers of whales", after watching groups of the animals hunt other large whales. Today, they are often called "orcas".

Harp seal

Pods
Killer whales live in small groups, or "pods". Each pod is a family, often with all the parents, children, grandparents, aunts and uncles living and travelling together. There are between 4 and 40 killer whales in a typical pod, but sometimes there are many more.

Hunting salmon
Killer whales hunt in packs, like wolves. They work together, often swimming in formation to trap and catch their prey, and reaching speeds of up to 50kph (30mph) when going in for the kill. Some packs like to eat fish, and they rarely eat anything else. Others prefer to eat meat such as seals.

Some killer whales like to eat salmon

Female killer whale
The female killer whale looks similar to the male but is considerably smaller - at about 3 tonnes, weighing roughly half his weight, and rarely growing longer than 7m (23ft). But she tends to live much longer and may reach a ripe old age of 80 years.

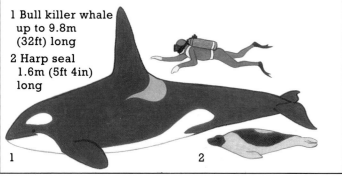

1 Bull killer whale up to 9.8m (32ft) long

2 Harp seal 1.6m (5ft 4in) long

People are the only creatures killer whales need to fear because we kill them, or capture them for zoos and safari parks

It is a mystery why killer whales do not hunt people, even though many of them eat seals and other large animals

Hunting seals
Killer whales have developed some clever techniques for catching seals. Sometimes, particularly in the Arctic and the Antarctic, they watch for the animals resting on pieces of floating ice and tip them into the water, often into the mouths of other members of the pod.

Dorsal fins
Towering above the female's curved and rather shark-like fin, the huge, triangular dorsal fin of the bull killer whale can reach a remarkable height of 1.8m (6ft), or roughly as tall as a man. It makes the killer whale an easy animal to spot.

Baby
A baby killer whale is a surprisingly large animal, measuring between 2.1m (6ft 10in) and 2.7m (8ft 10in) long when it is first born. It feeds on its mother's milk for at least a year after birth and may live with her family, or pod, for the rest of its life.

A large appetite
Some killer whales are not very keen on fish and prefer to hunt prey such as squid, turtles, penguins, seals, dolphins and even other whales. They have huge appetites. One male killer whale was found to have no fewer than 13 porpoises and 14 seals in its stomach. The male is enormous, reaching 9.8m (32ft) in length and weighing up to 8 tonnes. He may live as long as 50 years.

DIVE, DIVE, DIVE

Fish are able to breathe underwater because they have gills. But whales are different. Like people, they have lungs, which only work in the air. This means that, although they spend most of their time underwater, they have to return to the surface at frequent intervals to breathe. Sometimes, after long dives, they are so desperate for fresh air that they head for the surface like torpedos, shooting out of the water, then falling back in with a tremendous splash. They rest there for a while, taking a few deep breaths to recover, before diving once again.

Whales cannot breathe through their mouths, but take in air through their nostrils, or "blowholes". These are on the top of the head, so the animals can relax in the water with only a tiny part of their bodies showing above the surface. Most of the larger whales have two blowholes, but the sperm whale is unusual in having only one.

Sperm whale
One of the strangest of all the great whales is the sperm whale, a huge animal that seems to think it is a submarine. The male, which is larger than the female, can grow to 18m (59ft) in length and may weigh as much as 50 tonnes. Sperm whales are world champion divers and dive for longer, and deeper, than any other mammal in the world.

Tail dive
Whenever a sperm whale throws its tail high into the air, it is about to do a long, deep dive. The tail slides into the water, as its owner drops almost vertically to the murky depths below. The sperm whale's tail is easy to recognize because it is broad and powerful with a straight edge and a tiny "V" cut in the middle.

Dive sequence
There is an old rule of thumb, used by whalers many years ago, which says that for every metre of a sperm whale's length, it will breathe just over three times at the surface and spend a little more than three minutes underwater during its next dive.

1 A 15m (49ft) sperm whale takes about 50 breaths at the surface before diving

2 It dives for a total of 50 minutes

3 It begins to rise from the freezing cold, dark depths

4 As it breaks the surface, its nose and long, blunt head appear first

Moby Dick
The sperm whale is most famous for its starring role in the classic 19th century novel, *Moby Dick*. Written by Herman Melville, an American who was once a whaler himself, this is the story of a mythical great white sperm whale pursued across the seas by a ship full of sailors and whalers. The novel ends with a three-day battle in which almost everyone is killed. In real life, sperm whales have head-butted whaling vessels when they were attacked, and ships have bumped into whales resting peacefully on the surface.

Deep divers
It is difficult to measure how deep sperm whales dive. Large males have been recorded at depths of at least 2,250m (7,381ft). But there is some evidence to suggest that sperm whales can go even deeper, to more than 3km (nearly 2 miles) below the surface, holding their breath for two hours or more.

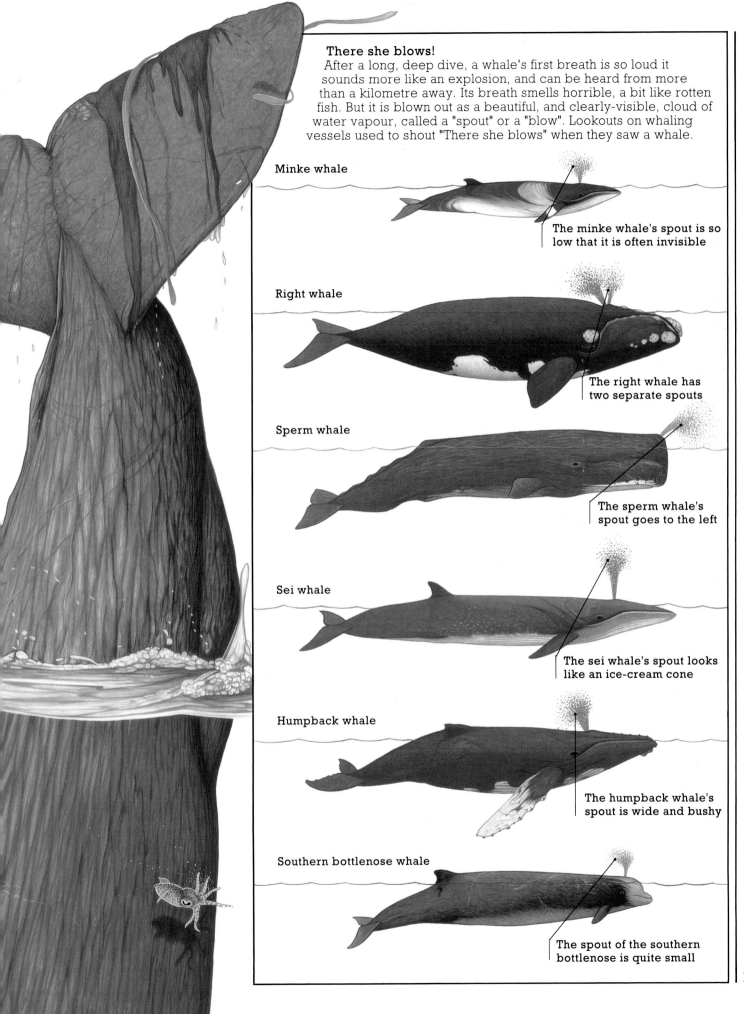

There she blows!

After a long, deep dive, a whale's first breath is so loud it sounds more like an explosion, and can be heard from more than a kilometre away. Its breath smells horrible, a bit like rotten fish. But it is blown out as a beautiful, and clearly-visible, cloud of water vapour, called a "spout" or a "blow". Lookouts on whaling vessels used to shout "There she blows" when they saw a whale.

Minke whale

The minke whale's spout is so low that it is often invisible

Right whale

The right whale has two separate spouts

Sperm whale

The sperm whale's spout goes to the left

Sei whale

The sei whale's spout looks like an ice-cream cone

Humpback whale

The humpback whale's spout is wide and bushy

Southern bottlenose whale

The spout of the southern bottlenose is quite small

19

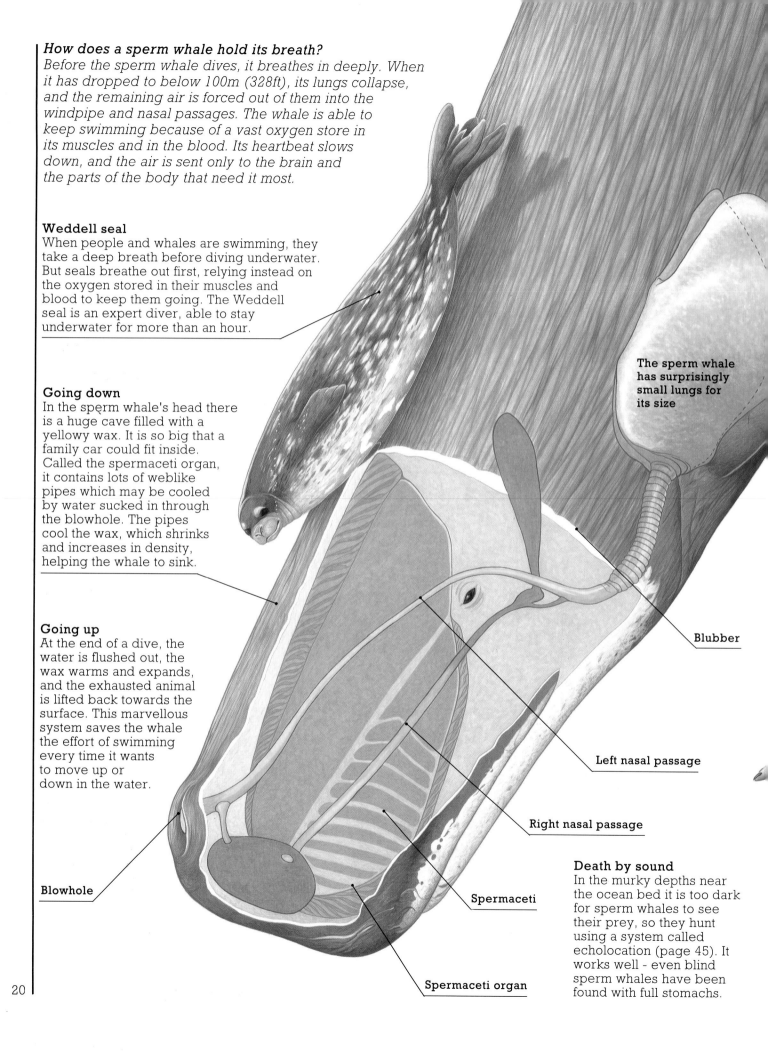

How does a sperm whale hold its breath?
Before the sperm whale dives, it breathes in deeply. When it has dropped to below 100m (328ft), its lungs collapse, and the remaining air is forced out of them into the windpipe and nasal passages. The whale is able to keep swimming because of a vast oxygen store in its muscles and in the blood. Its heartbeat slows down, and the air is sent only to the brain and the parts of the body that need it most.

Weddell seal
When people and whales are swimming, they take a deep breath before diving underwater. But seals breathe out first, relying instead on the oxygen stored in their muscles and blood to keep them going. The Weddell seal is an expert diver, able to stay underwater for more than an hour.

Going down
In the sperm whale's head there is a huge cave filled with a yellowy wax. It is so big that a family car could fit inside. Called the spermaceti organ, it contains lots of weblike pipes which may be cooled by water sucked in through the blowhole. The pipes cool the wax, which shrinks and increases in density, helping the whale to sink.

Going up
At the end of a dive, the water is flushed out, the wax warms and expands, and the exhausted animal is lifted back towards the surface. This marvellous system saves the whale the effort of swimming every time it wants to move up or down in the water.

The sperm whale has surprisingly small lungs for its size

Blubber

Left nasal passage

Right nasal passage

Spermaceti

Spermaceti organ

Blowhole

Death by sound
In the murky depths near the ocean bed it is too dark for sperm whales to see their prey, so they hunt using a system called echolocation (page 45). It works well - even blind sperm whales have been found with full stomachs.

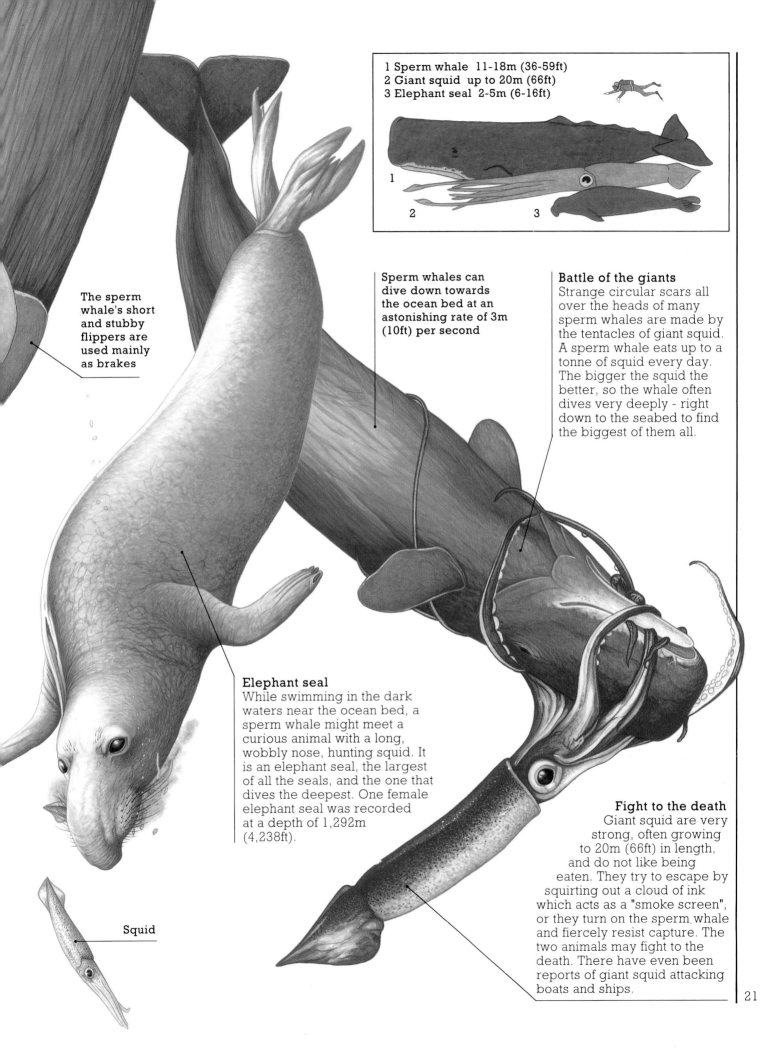

1 Sperm whale 11-18m (36-59ft)
2 Giant squid up to 20m (66ft)
3 Elephant seal 2-5m (6-16ft)

1

2   3

The sperm whale's short and stubby flippers are used mainly as brakes

Sperm whales can dive down towards the ocean bed at an astonishing rate of 3m (10ft) per second

Battle of the giants
Strange circular scars all over the heads of many sperm whales are made by the tentacles of giant squid. A sperm whale eats up to a tonne of squid every day. The bigger the squid the better, so the whale often dives very deeply - right down to the seabed to find the biggest of them all.

Elephant seal
While swimming in the dark waters near the ocean bed, a sperm whale might meet a curious animal with a long, wobbly nose, hunting squid. It is an elephant seal, the largest of all the seals, and the one that dives the deepest. One female elephant seal was recorded at a depth of 1,292m (4,238ft).

Squid

Fight to the death
Giant squid are very strong, often growing to 20m (66ft) in length, and do not like being eaten. They try to escape by squirting out a cloud of ink which acts as a "smoke screen", or they turn on the sperm whale and fiercely resist capture. The two animals may fight to the death. There have even been reports of giant squid attacking boats and ships.

PERSONAL APPEARANCE

Dolphins all belong to the same family, but they do not all look alike. As well as the obvious variations in colour and pattern, the shapes of their bodies, beaks, flippers and fins are also very different. In many species, they also change in appearance as they grow older. Young Risso's dolphins are light grey when they are first born, but soon become a chocolate-brown colour, later turning a silvery grey. Spotted dolphins near the coast tend to be larger than their relatives living far out to sea. The yellow patches on common dolphins may fade a little during the winter. Variations like these - and the fact that dolphins are always on the move - make them surprisingly difficult animals to identify at sea.

Dark above, light below
Many dolphins have light-coloured bellies and dark-coloured backs. This camouflage helps them blend into their surroundings. Looking at them from above, they are almost invisible against the dark ocean depths. When seen from below, they are difficult to make out against the brightness of the surface waters.

Spotted dolphin
One of the strangest things about spotted dolphins is that not all of them have spots. The number and size of spots varies according to where they live and how old they are. They are all born without them, but the first ones usually begin to appear when the babies are about a year old.

Rightwhale dolphin
One of the most graceful of all dolphins is the southern right whale dolphin, which lives in the cool waters of the southern hemisphere. Its back curves smoothly and evenly from the tip of its nose to the beginning of its tail, because it has no fin. It can still swim quite fast, probably using its flattened body to provide stability in the water.

Hourglass dolphin
These dolphins have "disruptive patterning". From a distance, several of them together look like a school of fish, so they can sneak up on their prey undetected. At close range, their short, thick beaks make them look as though they are blowing kisses.

Ganges river dolphin
The rather plump Ganges river dolphin is not brightly-coloured. This is because it lives in murky rivers, where elaborate patterns would be useless as no animal can see more than a few centimetres in front of its nose.

Indo-Pacific humpback dolphin
This strange-looking inhabitant of the Indian and Pacific Oceans really does have a camel-like hump on its back. A baby humpback is the classic dolphin shape, but the fatty hump begins to grow as it gets older. Strangely though, while the animals living west of Indonesia have very distinctive humps, those living in the east have no humps at all.

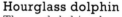

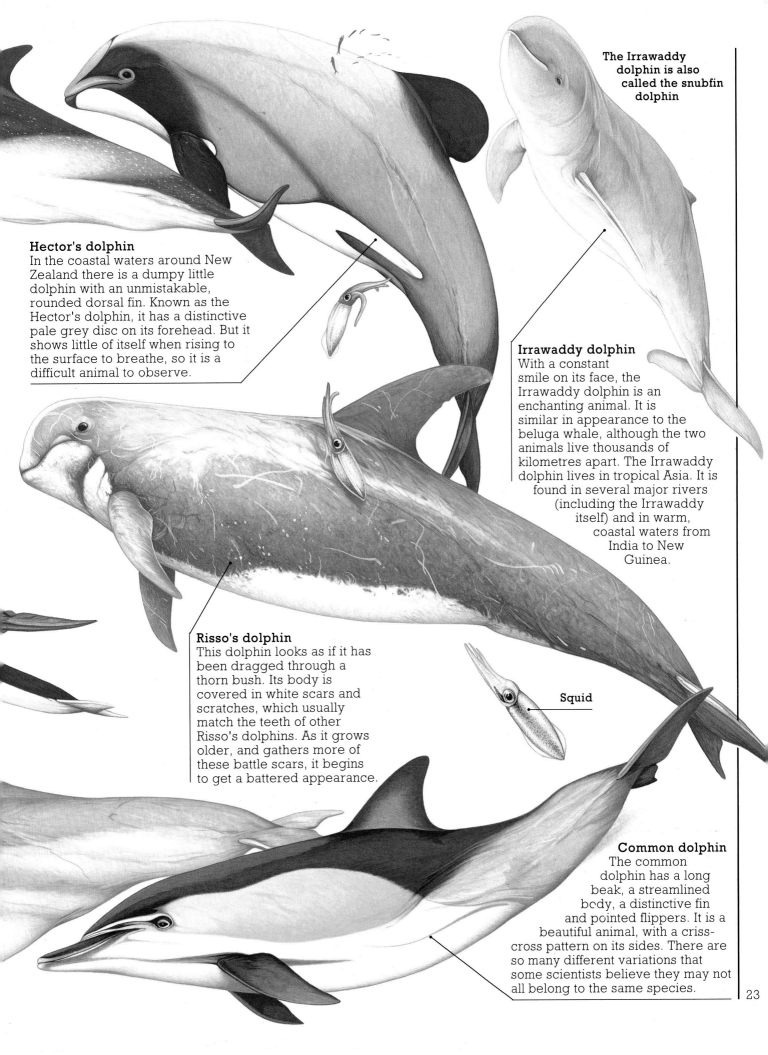

The Irrawaddy
dolphin is also
called the snubfin
dolphin

Hector's dolphin

In the coastal waters around New
Zealand there is a dumpy little
dolphin with an unmistakable,
rounded dorsal fin. Known as the
Hector's dolphin, it has a distinctive
pale grey disc on its forehead. But it
shows little of itself when rising to
the surface to breathe, so it is a
difficult animal to observe.

Irrawaddy dolphin

With a constant
smile on its face, the
Irrawaddy dolphin is an
enchanting animal. It is
similar in appearance to the
beluga whale, although the two
animals live thousands of
kilometres apart. The Irrawaddy
dolphin lives in tropical Asia. It is
found in several major rivers
(including the Irrawaddy
itself) and in warm,
coastal waters from
India to New
Guinea.

Risso's dolphin

This dolphin looks as if it has
been dragged through a
thorn bush. Its body is
covered in white scars and
scratches, which usually
match the teeth of other
Risso's dolphins. As it grows
older, and gathers more of
these battle scars, it begins
to get a battered appearance.

Squid

Common dolphin

The common
dolphin has a long
beak, a streamlined
body, a distinctive fin
and pointed flippers. It is a
beautiful animal, with a criss-
cross pattern on its sides. There are
so many different variations that
some scientists believe they may not
all belong to the same species.

CIRCUS OF THE SEAS

Whales and dolphins sometimes seem to spend as much time in the air as they do underwater. They turn somersaults, twist, jump in unison and poke their heads above the surface. Wild and free, they put on acrobatic displays that would shame many circus performers. Spotted dolphins, for example, leap so high that they appear to hang in mid-air before falling back with a splash. Dusky dolphins shoot out of the water at high speed and do a somersault head-over-tail. And some whales hold their tail flukes high in the air to catch the wind in order to sail. Many of these playful animals are good at imitating one another and, when one discovers a new manoeuvre, the others will try it as well. One bottlenose dolphin even copied a sleeping fur seal by swimming on its back with both flippers pressed flat against its belly. But the big question puzzling many scientists is whether there is a special reason for these games, or if the animals are simply having fun.

Showtime!

Many whales and dolphins will abandon shoals of tasty fish to join a passing boat or ship. They are real extroverts and cannot resist the chance to show off. They race over to play in the bow waves, or to perform spectacular acrobatic displays alongside the vessel as it cuts through the water. Some even roll on their sides to look at everyone on deck, just to make sure that they are being watched and that the spectators are enjoying the show.

Porpoising

Many dolphins and porpoises have found a marvellous way of travelling long distances without using up too much energy. Called "porpoising", it involves swimming in long, low leaps and enables the animals to breathe while travelling at high speed. Northern right whale dolphins are experts at porpoising. They usually leap in a graceful arc together - looking like acrobats or dancers.

Surfing

Commerson's dolphins usually live in shallow water near the coast. They are keen surfers and spend much of their time riding the waves, or practising their manoeuvres in the backwash of passing ships. Several of them surf together and they can often be seen speeding along the length of a wave as it rolls into the shore. When the wave breaks, they swim out to wait for the next one - just like human surfers.

Breaching
The Bryde's whale (pronounced "bree-dahs") sometimes launches itself into the air like a rocket and falls back in the water with a tremendous splash. This strange behaviour is called "breaching" (pages 48-49). It is a popular pastime among many of the great whales and some go on "breaching binges", doing dozens of breaches within a few minutes of each other.

Splashing
Some dolphins seem to enjoy any game that makes a splash. A large herd of Pacific white-sided dolphins makes such a disturbance in the water that their splashes can often be seen long before they actually come into view.

Spinning
Spinner dolphins are the acrobatic champions of the dolphin world. They will do anything to draw attention to their antics, but one of their favourite tricks is to spin around sideways. They hurl themselves into the air and spin over and over several times in a single leap. Most of their spinning is done in the evening, while they prepare for their night-time feed.

Riding bow waves
This white-beaked dolphin is getting a free ride by swimming immediately in front of a boat. It is being pushed along through the water. Many dolphins love the challenge of modern high-speed boats, and squeal excitedly when they find a fast one.

Spyhopping
The pygmy killer whale does not seem to breach, approach boats or surf. But, every so often, it kicks furiously with its tail and pokes its head and part of its body out of the water. This is called "spyhopping" and enables the whale to "spy" on its surroundings. It can stay there for half a minute or more.

25

MOVING ABOUT

Whales are nearly always on the move, seeking out food or finding suitable places in which to breed. Some travel only at specific times of the year, others simply move around according to local conditions. Many patrol small home ranges, while a few undertake long and arduous journeys across some of the world's largest oceans. Pilot whales often move with migrating squid, for example, and narwhals according to the formation and break-up of the Arctic ice. But the greatest travellers of all are the great whales. They spend many months of the year travelling between their feeding and breeding grounds. Usually, they migrate towards the poles in summer, to feed in the rich waters there, and in winter swim towards the warm, calm waters of the tropics to have their young.

Always on the move
Grey whales are famous for their long migrations. They spend all winter at their breeding grounds at Baja California, in Mexico. Then, in the spring, they head north for their summer feeding grounds in the rich waters of the Arctic Ocean, off the coast of Alaska. On the way, they hug the North American coastline, often swimming very close to the shore.

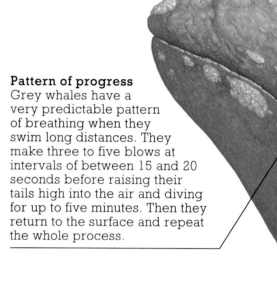

Travelling giants
Grey whales are huge animals, growing up to 15m (49ft) long and weighing as much as 35 tonnes. Their tongues alone weigh the same as a small family car. On migration, a grey whale swims up to 20,000km (12,500 miles) every year. In a grey whale's typical lifetime of 40 years, this is equivalent to a return trip to the Moon.

Pattern of progress
Grey whales have a very predictable pattern of breathing when they swim long distances. They make three to five blows at intervals of between 15 and 20 seconds before raising their tails high into the air and diving for up to five minutes. Then they return to the surface and repeat the whole process.

Giving birth

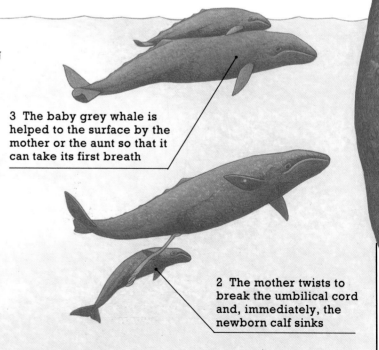

Grey whales mate in the warm waters off the coast of Mexico and, by the time they return the following year, the females are ready to give birth. Their babies are born in shallow lagoons, usually in water less than 10m (32ft) deep. Grey whales rarely give birth unassisted. There is usually an "aunt" - another female - ready to help.

3 The baby grey whale is helped to the surface by the mother or the aunt so that it can take its first breath

1 The 5m (16ft) baby grey whale, which weighs almost a tonne, is born tail-first, like all other cetaceans

2 The mother twists to break the umbilical cord and, immediately, the newborn calf sinks

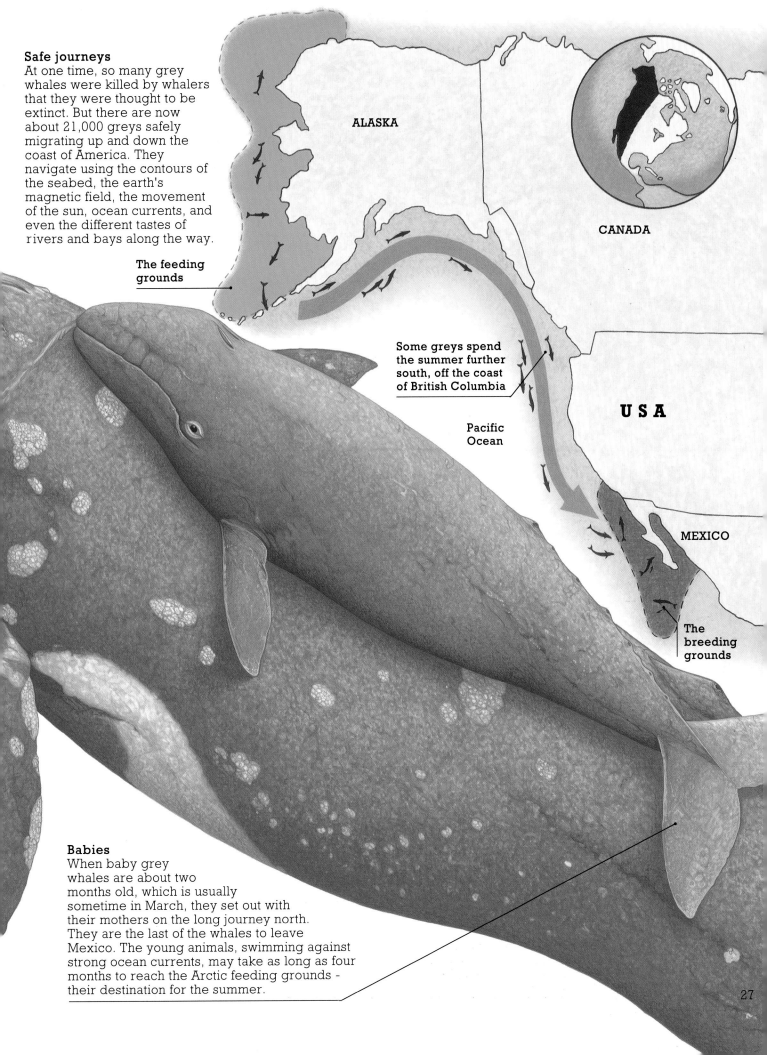

Safe journeys
At one time, so many grey whales were killed by whalers that they were thought to be extinct. But there are now about 21,000 greys safely migrating up and down the coast of America. They navigate using the contours of the seabed, the earth's magnetic field, the movement of the sun, ocean currents, and even the different tastes of rivers and bays along the way.

The feeding grounds

ALASKA

CANADA

Some greys spend the summer further south, off the coast of British Columbia

Pacific Ocean

USA

MEXICO

The breeding grounds

Babies
When baby grey whales are about two months old, which is usually sometime in March, they set out with their mothers on the long journey north. They are the last of the whales to leave Mexico. The young animals, swimming against strong ocean currents, may take as long as four months to reach the Arctic feeding grounds - their destination for the summer.

LIVING TOGETHER

Most whales, dolphins and porpoises do not like being alone. Some species enjoy each other's company so much that they gather in enormous herds of several thousand animals. If there are sharks or killer whales around, it is often safer to travel in these "gangs" - and it is easier to find food with everyone searching together. But group sizes depend on the animals and where they live, or even on the time of day.

Members of a group usually look after one another. They shout warnings of impending danger, push injured companions to the surface to breathe, and try to help if one of them is in trouble. Sometimes, of course, there are squabbles and disagreements - just like in human societies. Males fight over females and, since most groups have strict pecking orders, the animals chase, ram, bite or slap one another to sort out who is boss.

Family groups
Whales, dolphins and porpoises living together are often closely related. Some species live with children, parents, grandparents, aunts and uncles. Other groups are formed by strangers at the best feeding and breeding grounds.

Beluga whales
More than 1,000 belugas sometimes gather at their summer haunts but, even in such large groups, the mothers and their calves stay side-by-side. Twins are very rare and, when two babies are born together, the mother can seldom provide enough milk to keep them both alive.

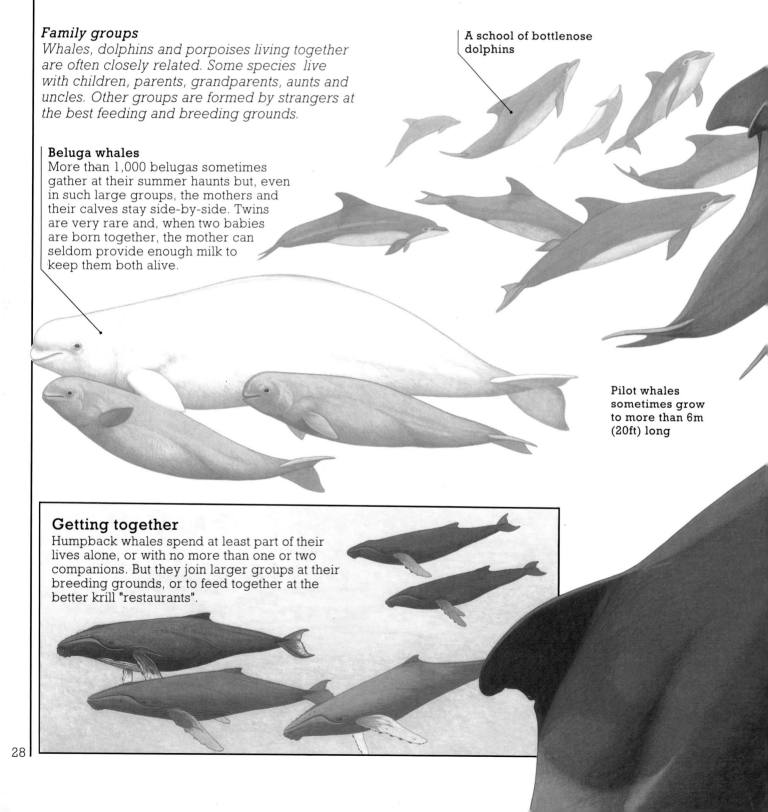

A school of bottlenose dolphins

Pilot whales sometimes grow to more than 6m (20ft) long

Getting together
Humpback whales spend at least part of their lives alone, or with no more than one or two companions. But they join larger groups at their breeding grounds, or to feed together at the better krill "restaurants".

Getting on

When we grow old our skin becomes wrinkled. But grey whales are born with wrinkles, and these gradually disappear as the years pass. The young animals look quite different to their parents. They are much darker in colour and have a smooth skin, whereas the adults are heavily mottled with barnacles and scars.

The white, yellow or orange patches on older animals are caused by whale lice

A friend in need

These two bottlenose dolphins are lifting an injured companion to the surface to breathe. They will look after it for hours, or days, if necessary. There are many stories of them helping people in a similar way, although no one is sure whether these are real acts of kindness. They may be simply cases of mistaken identity.

Sticking together

The strongest bond of all is the one between a mother and her calf. Baby whales and dolphins often remain so close to their mothers that the two animals sometimes appear to be stuck together with glue.

Head-banging

Some whales and dolphins have very strange ways of showing how much they like each other. When male and female shortfin pilot whales are courting, they are thought to bang their heads together underwater. These violent collisions must be quite painful.

29

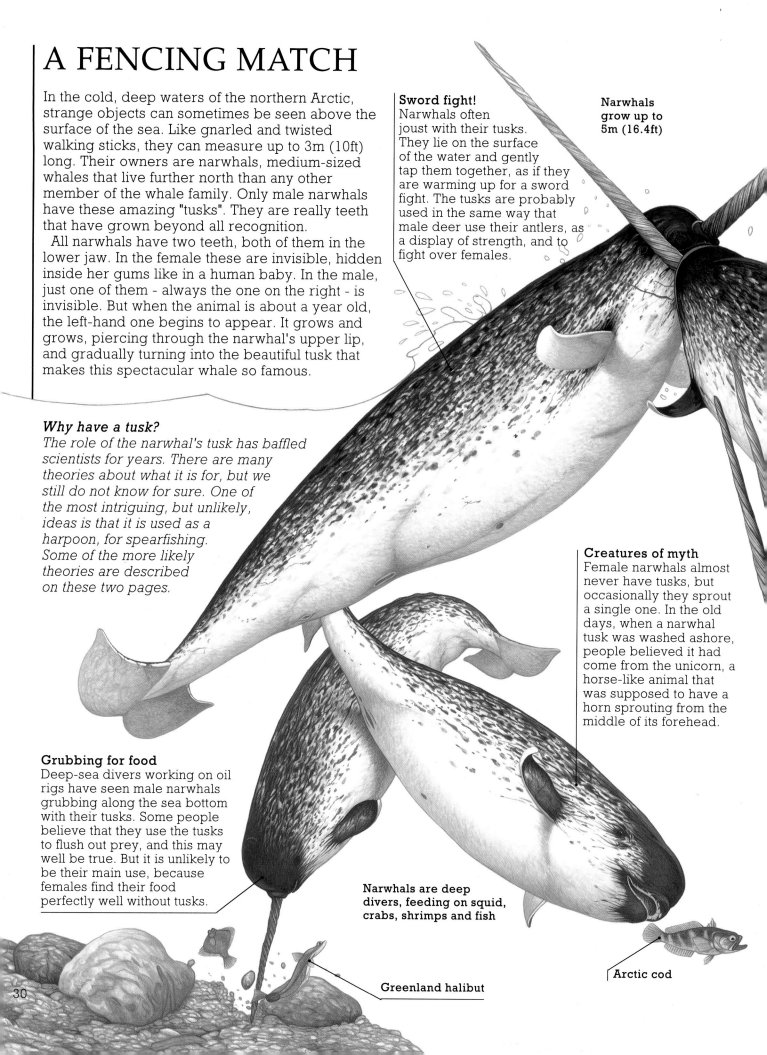

A FENCING MATCH

In the cold, deep waters of the northern Arctic, strange objects can sometimes be seen above the surface of the sea. Like gnarled and twisted walking sticks, they can measure up to 3m (10ft) long. Their owners are narwhals, medium-sized whales that live further north than any other member of the whale family. Only male narwhals have these amazing "tusks". They are really teeth that have grown beyond all recognition.

All narwhals have two teeth, both of them in the lower jaw. In the female these are invisible, hidden inside her gums like in a human baby. In the male, just one of them - always the one on the right - is invisible. But when the animal is about a year old, the left-hand one begins to appear. It grows and grows, piercing through the narwhal's upper lip, and gradually turning into the beautiful tusk that makes this spectacular whale so famous.

Why have a tusk?
The role of the narwhal's tusk has baffled scientists for years. There are many theories about what it is for, but we still do not know for sure. One of the most intriguing, but unlikely, ideas is that it is used as a harpoon, for spearfishing. Some of the more likely theories are described on these two pages.

Sword fight!
Narwhals often joust with their tusks. They lie on the surface of the water and gently tap them together, as if they are warming up for a sword fight. The tusks are probably used in the same way that male deer use their antlers, as a display of strength, and to fight over females.

Narwhals grow up to 5m (16.4ft)

Creatures of myth
Female narwhals almost never have tusks, but occasionally they sprout a single one. In the old days, when a narwhal tusk was washed ashore, people believed it had come from the unicorn, a horse-like animal that was supposed to have a horn sprouting from the middle of its forehead.

Grubbing for food
Deep-sea divers working on oil rigs have seen male narwhals grubbing along the sea bottom with their tusks. Some people believe that they use the tusks to flush out prey, and this may well be true. But it is unlikely to be their main use, because females find their food perfectly well without tusks.

Narwhals are deep divers, feeding on squid, crabs, shrimps and fish

Arctic cod

Greenland halibut

Room to breathe
In cold weather, narwhals sometimes find themselves trapped underneath ice. They are likely to drown unless they can find a breathing-hole nearby, or can make a new one. But they treat their tusks with care and prefer to use their foreheads instead to head-butt through ice up to 18cm (7in) thick.

Icy quarrels
Where reliable breathing-holes are in short supply, narwhals and walruses have been seen squabbling over them. Yet walruses are capable of killing large animals, such as seals, and have been known to eat narwhals. Some experts believe that the whales may use their tusks to defend themselves.

Jousting whales appear to be playing but the "game" is serious

Double tusked
A small number of male narwhals have two tusks. They are both straight, and they spiral in an anti-clockwise direction. But the extra right-hand tusk is usually shorter than the main one. Many males have broken tusks, and they are often badly scarred.

Weird teeth
The male strap-toothed beaked whale has only two teeth. These grow from the lower jaw, curling upwards and backwards and over the top of its upper jaw. In older animals, the teeth sometimes grow to a length of 30cm (12in) or more, and meet in the middle. They act like a muzzle, preventing the whales from opening their mouths properly. Surprisingly, they can still catch their favourite food, squid, by using their mouths like vacuum cleaners.

Many male strap-toothed beaked whales have cuts and scratches on their faces, which seem to have been made by others males

The "strap tooth"

31

EARLY DAYS

When a whale or dolphin is born, it experiences the greatest shock of its life. Having spent many months in the warmth and safety of its mother's body, it is suddenly propelled into a new home where it feels very cold and wet. In this rather hostile environment, it is unable to breathe and, almost immediately, starts to sink. But the baby is in no danger because its mother, or another member of the group, is there to help during those first bewildering moments of life. Few births have been seen in the wild, but it is known that, unlike most other mammals, whales and dolphins usually have just one baby at a time. Adults are patient and understanding when the baby is being playful or mischievous. They protect it from predators and, as it grows older, they teach it to find food. But it is many months, or even years, before the young animal is ready to fend for itself.

Bottlenose dolphins
There is some evidence to suggest that some larger whales are born head-first, just like land mammals. But most members of the family probably come out tail-first. This is certainly true of young bottlenose dolphins, which have been studied in more detail than most other species.

1 Giving birth
A baby bottlenose dolphin is born after a year inside its mother's womb. About 1m (3ft) long, it looks like a miniature version of its parents. It is usually born in shallow water, so the mother and her new baby can easily come up for air.

During the birth, the mother may be attended by a "friend", known as an "aunt", who helps with the birth and also in caring for the baby in the months to come

In the womb
The growth and development of young whales and dolphins is very similar to human babies. But, while a human baby is born after only nine months, cetaceans are usually inside their mothers' wombs for much longer - up to 12 months in baleen whales and as long as 18 months in some toothed whales. Whales and dolphins have to grow surprisingly quickly. A blue whale calf, for example, reaches a length of more than 7m (23ft) in just one year. The seven-week-old embryo of this white-sided dolphin already has a small tail and its flippers are beginning to form. The unborn human baby is also seven weeks old and little more than 10mm (less than an inch) long, but can already bend its elbows and move its hands.

The embryo of a white-sided dolphin at seven weeks

The embryo of a human baby at seven weeks

32

Growth rings

It is very difficult to measure the age of a whale or dolphin. But the teeth of many species give some fairly accurate clues. When a tooth is cut in half, a series of layers, rather like the growth rings of a tree, are revealed in the middle. Broadly speaking, one complete band in the tooth is the same as one ring in the tree - and equal to a year of growth. This sperm whale's tooth has 23 narrow bands and 23 broad bands, which means that its owner was 23 years old.

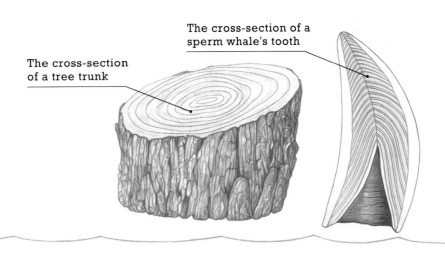

The cross-section of a sperm whale's tooth

The cross-section of a tree trunk

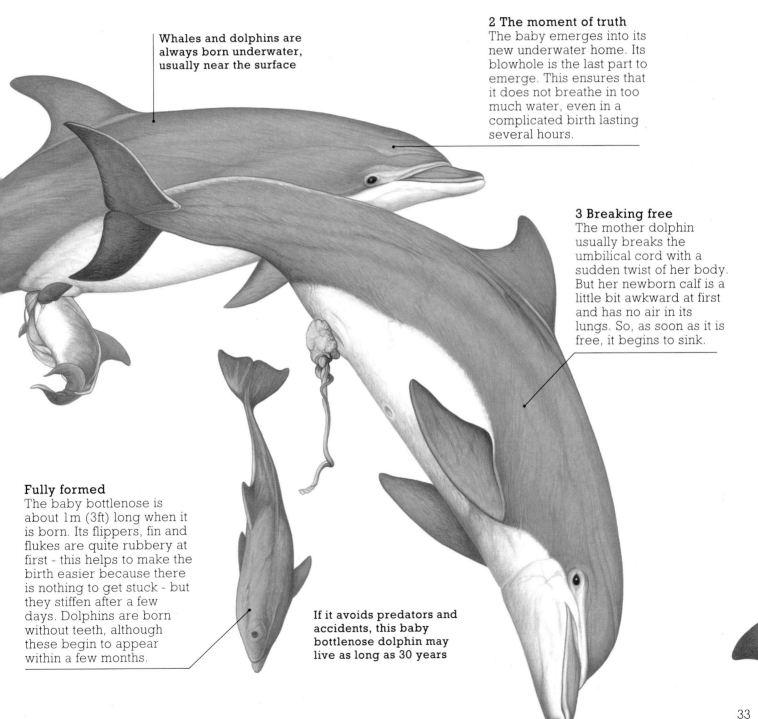

Whales and dolphins are always born underwater, usually near the surface

2 The moment of truth

The baby emerges into its new underwater home. Its blowhole is the last part to emerge. This ensures that it does not breathe in too much water, even in a complicated birth lasting several hours.

3 Breaking free

The mother dolphin usually breaks the umbilical cord with a sudden twist of her body. But her newborn calf is a little bit awkward at first and has no air in its lungs. So, as soon as it is free, it begins to sink.

Fully formed

The baby bottlenose is about 1m (3ft) long when it is born. Its flippers, fin and flukes are quite rubbery at first - this helps to make the birth easier because there is nothing to get stuck - but they stiffen after a few days. Dolphins are born without teeth, although these begin to appear within a few months.

If it avoids predators and accidents, this baby bottlenose dolphin may live as long as 30 years

33

Doting mothers

Mother dolphins fuss over their babies and keep an eye on them every minute of the day and night. Even the other adults in the herd have an inexhaustible supply of patience while the boisterous youngsters head-butt them, poke them, race around and generally behave like spoilt children. The bond between a mother and her calf is incredibly strong and their movements are perfectly coordinated. When she turns the baby turns, when she dives the baby dives, and when she surfaces to breathe the baby does the same.

5 Taking breath

If all goes well, the calf does not try to breathe underwater. If it did, it could take in a lungful of water and drown. But, as soon as it breaks through the surface, its blowhole automatically opens up and it can safely take in its first breath of air.

4 Reaching the air

The mother and an assistant are ready to help the newborn calf. Within a few seconds of being born, the baby is nudged towards the surface of the water to breathe. It soon gains confidence and, in about half an hour, can swim around quite happily on its own.

Another female dolphin may help the baby to the surface - not the father, as the males have very little, if anything, to do with looking after their young

Shark attack

Few dolphins will tolerate sharks around when they are looking after their young. Some species are famous for the ferocity with which they fight off attackers. This bottlenose dolphin is killing a whitetip reef shark by ramming the shark's soft belly with its snout.

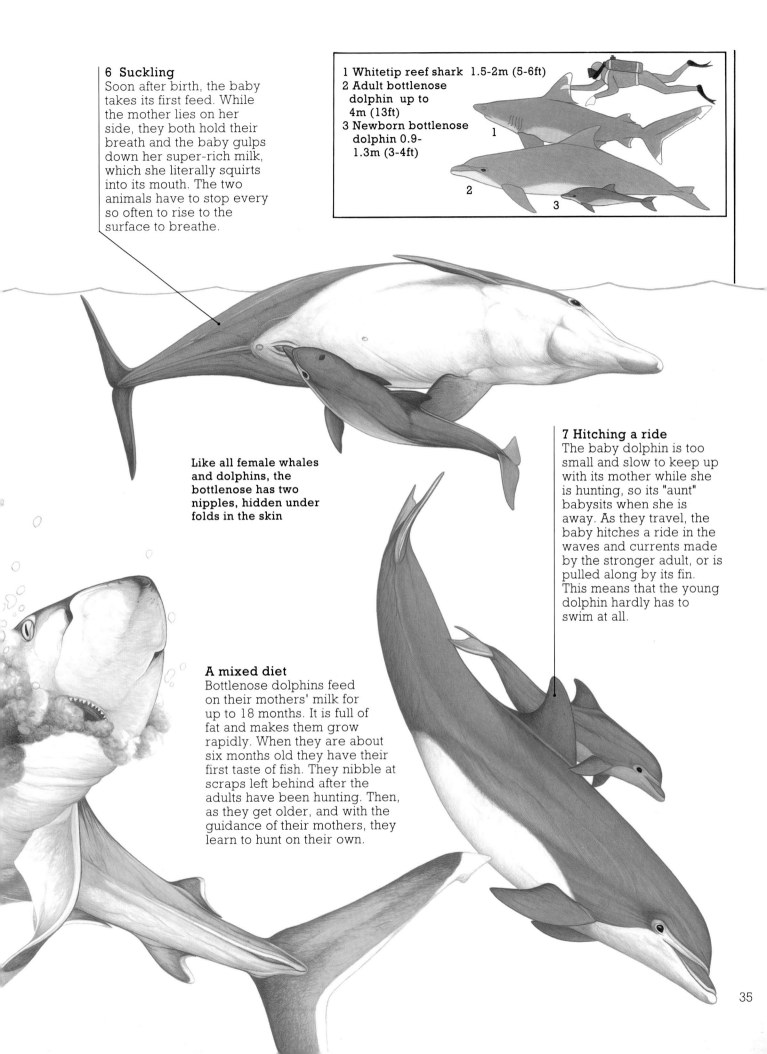

6 Suckling
Soon after birth, the baby takes its first feed. While the mother lies on her side, they both hold their breath and the baby gulps down her super-rich milk, which she literally squirts into its mouth. The two animals have to stop every so often to rise to the surface to breathe.

1 Whitetip reef shark 1.5-2m (5-6ft)
2 Adult bottlenose dolphin up to 4m (13ft)
3 Newborn bottlenose dolphin 0.9-1.3m (3-4ft)

Like all female whales and dolphins, the bottlenose has two nipples, hidden under folds in the skin

7 Hitching a ride
The baby dolphin is too small and slow to keep up with its mother while she is hunting, so its "aunt" babysits when she is away. As they travel, the baby hitches a ride in the waves and currents made by the stronger adult, or is pulled along by its fin. This means that the young dolphin hardly has to swim at all.

A mixed diet
Bottlenose dolphins feed on their mothers' milk for up to 18 months. It is full of fat and makes them grow rapidly. When they are about six months old they have their first taste of fish. They nibble at scraps left behind after the adults have been hunting. Then, as they get older, and with the guidance of their mothers, they learn to hunt on their own.

ATTACK AND DEFENCE

Swimming in the sea can be a risky business. People are the greatest threat to whales, dolphins and porpoises, but there are a number of other dangerous creatures which they need to avoid. Pygmy and false killer whales, and pilot whales, sometimes eat the smaller members of the family. There are even reports of dolphins being drowned by octopuses, which smother their blowholes when they themselves are under attack. Large whales are generally much safer. But the two enemies they all try to avoid are sharks and killer whales.

No animal in the sea is safe from killer whale attack, although dolphins and porpoises make particularly easy prey when the killers herd them like sheep into tightly-packed groups. Large whales under attack defend themselves by lashing out with their powerful flukes or thumping the attackers with their flippers. One right whale managed to throw a killer whale 10m (33ft) into the air with a single swipe of its tail.

A near miss!
It is not unusual to see whales and dolphins with bits missing. Chunks bitten out of their tails, torn flippers and nasty-looking scars may all be evidence of their narrow escapes from predators. In one study off the coast of Canada, a third of all the humpback whales in the area showed scarring and other damage caused by killer whale attacks.

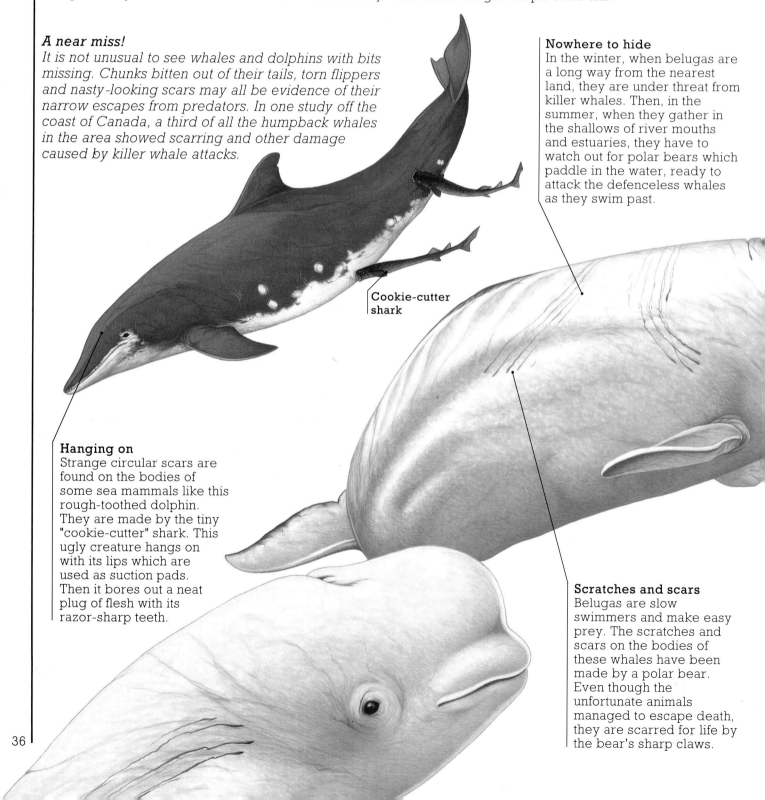

Cookie-cutter shark

Nowhere to hide
In the winter, when belugas are a long way from the nearest land, they are under threat from killer whales. Then, in the summer, when they gather in the shallows of river mouths and estuaries, they have to watch out for polar bears which paddle in the water, ready to attack the defenceless whales as they swim past.

Hanging on
Strange circular scars are found on the bodies of some sea mammals like this rough-toothed dolphin. They are made by the tiny "cookie-cutter" shark. This ugly creature hangs on with its lips which are used as suction pads. Then it bores out a neat plug of flesh with its razor-sharp teeth.

Scratches and scars
Belugas are slow swimmers and make easy prey. The scratches and scars on the bodies of these whales have been made by a polar bear. Even though the unfortunate animals managed to escape death, they are scarred for life by the bear's sharp claws.

Trapped!

In the winter, beluga whales sometimes get trapped in small holes in the ice. Unable to hold their breath for long enough to find the open sea, they have to wait for the ice to clear. Not surprisingly, polar bears make the most of their misfortune and pounce on them from the ice-edge or haul the whales out one by one.

There may be dozens of belugas crowded together and they find it hard to escape

A good appetite

Polar bears normally eat ringed and bearded seals, but they are powerful animals and will feed on almost anything when the opportunity arises. Beluga whales sometimes appear on the menu.

Polar bears have thick hair, instead of blubber, to help them keep warm

Polar bears are excellent swimmers

Deadly blow

A polar bear can kill a large animal with a single swipe of its paw. It finds beluga whales, which grow to 4.5m (15ft) long, easy prey, and will tackle them from the ice pack (see above) or by attacking underwater.

Killing pack

Killer whales have been known to eat at least 24 different species of cetaceans - from tiny dolphins to the giant of all giants, the blue whale. They rarely tackle large whales if they are travelling in groups, but stragglers, such as this one, are always at risk. Having surrounded the frightened animal, the killer whales are lunging at it from all directions, biting out chunks of flesh. At the same time, they force it to stay underwater until eventually it drowns. The killers eat only the tongue, the skin and the lips of a whale. After they have eaten their fill, everything else is left for sea scavengers, such as gulls and skuas, to clear up.

This pod of killer whales is making a frenzied attack on a 21m (69ft) fin whale

GROWING UP

A female whale or dolphin has to work very hard. From the moment she is old enough to breed until the day she dies, she spends most of her life either carrying a new baby in her womb, or caring for a calf by her side. Some species even give birth to babies which are almost half the length of themselves. Then the babies need feeding and constant attention for months - or even years - before they are able to survive in the cold and dangerous underwater world on their own.

There are very few species of whale in which the females are able to relax in their old age. However, there is one exception. Female pilot whales live for many years after their last babies are born and are respected by other members of the family group, just as in some human societies. But even they have to make themselves useful by babysitting, and by passing on their knowledge and experience to other members of the group.

Like parent, like child
Many species give birth to tiny versions of themselves. Baby white-sided, bottlenose and common dolphins, for example, all look identical to the adults - they are just smaller and less well-behaved. Baby blue whales also look like their parents. They are exactly the same shape and bluish grey colour and, apart from their size, are almost impossible to tell apart.

After ten months inside its mother's womb, a baby blue whale weighs about half a tonne

Newborn calf
In the two months before a baby blue whale is born, its weight increases by two tonnes. This is about 1,000 times faster than the growth of a human baby in the womb. The newborn whale is 6 to 7m (20 to 23ft) long and almost an exact copy of its parents.

Two months old
The mother whale gives her calf great care and attention. The baby drinks about 200 litres (44 gallons) of the rich milk provided by its mother every day. It grows at an astonishing rate - gaining as much as 4kg (9lb) in weight every hour.

Seven months old
After seven months, the whale reaches a length of 15m (49ft), or two-thirds the size of its mother. The milk supply is poorer by now, so it has to become independent. This happens at the feeding grounds, where the young whale can eat as much as it needs.

After the young whale begins to find its own food, it is another nine or ten years before it reaches 19-24m (62-79ft) and is able to breed

1 Adult blue whale male: 25m (82ft) female: 26m (86ft)
2 Newborn blue whale 6-7m (20-23ft)

Nature's giants
Blue whales do not stop growing until they are 25-30 years old. Females are slightly larger than males of the same age. The longest ever recorded was an incredible 33.58m (110ft) female, although their average length is 26m (85ft).

Changing with age
In some species, such as beluga whales, bridled dolphins and Atlantic humpback dolphins, the young animals do not look like their parents. Some of them are a different colour when they are born and others are a different shape. But they all change gradually as they grow older.

Spotty?
The bridled dolphin is born without spots. But spots begin to appear as it grows older - first on its head and belly, then gradually over the rest of its body. The spots become bigger and more numerous with age.

As the bridled dolphin grows older, its light and dark patterning also becomes more intricate

Getting the hump
The Atlantic humpback dolphin is famous for the small camel-like hump in the middle of its back. But its young calf does not have a hump at all and looks like any other species of dolphin.

AT PLAY

It is impossible not to be intrigued by the curiosity and playfulness of whales and dolphins. They are full of high spirits. They chase one another, jump in the air, splash their tails and flippers, roll over, and play with things in the water. Sometimes they swim along in pairs, touching flippers as if they are holding hands. Some, such as the bottlenose dolphin, even "walk" on their tails, kicking furiously to keep most of their bodies out of the water for several seconds at a time. They seem to enjoy challenging themselves and, if anyone is watching, like nothing more than to show off in front of an audience. But play is useful as well as fun. It encourages different members of a herd to get to know one another, which may be important when they are hunting together or avoiding a predator. It also helps young animals to learn and practise some of the skills they will need later in life.

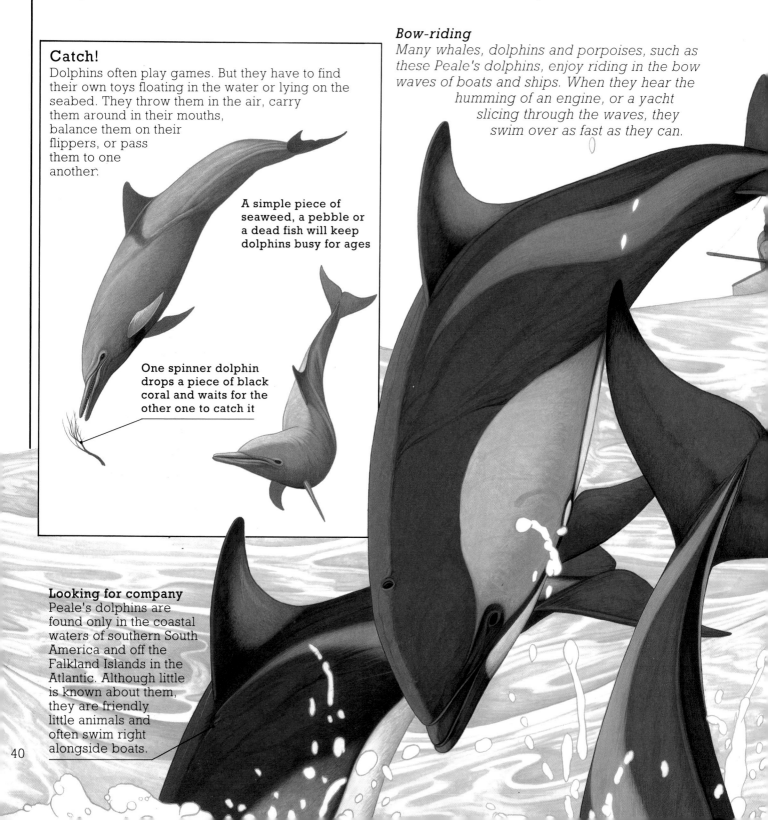

Catch!

Dolphins often play games. But they have to find their own toys floating in the water or lying on the seabed. They throw them in the air, carry them around in their mouths, balance them on their flippers, or pass them to one another.

A simple piece of seaweed, a pebble or a dead fish will keep dolphins busy for ages

One spinner dolphin drops a piece of black coral and waits for the other one to catch it

Bow-riding
Many whales, dolphins and porpoises, such as these Peale's dolphins, enjoy riding in the bow waves of boats and ships. When they hear the humming of an engine, or a yacht slicing through the waves, they swim over as fast as they can.

Looking for company
Peale's dolphins are found only in the coastal waters of southern South America and off the Falkland Islands in the Atlantic. Although little is known about them, they are friendly little animals and often swim right alongside boats.

Friendlies

Some dolphins enjoy the company of people and other animals. They are usually called "friendlies" and may come back to the same place day after day to play games or to be tickled. Some of them to prefer playing with children, although adults are always welcome to join in. Others will even let their human friends hang onto their dorsal fins to hitch an underwater ride. This bottlenose dolphin is playing a game with some Galapagos sealions.

The other sealion playfully nips the dolphin's tail

One of the sealions plays tug-of-war with a piece of seaweed

It is the movement of the boat through the water that attracts the dolphins to play

1 Galapagos sealion up to 2.2m (7ft 3in)
2 Bottlenose dolphin up to 3.9m (12ft 9in)
3 Peale's dolphin up to 2.2m (7ft 3in)
4 Spinner dolphin up to 2.1m (6ft 9in)

In search of adventure

Some whales and dolphins prefer small boats to big ones because they can get up to mischief by splashing the people on board. But others get bored if a boat is moving too slowly and usually leave in search of a more exciting way to pass the time.

Putting on a show

As the dolphins approach a boat, they put on an impressive display of acrobatics, leaping in the air and twisting and turning. Then they swim alongside, or right at the front, boisterously zig-zagging and splashing about. Sometimes they keep the boat company for an hour before getting fed up and swimming away as suddenly as they appeared.

PORPOISES

Many dolphins are terrible show-offs. They like to attract attention to themselves by leaping high into the air, or swimming alongside boats and playing in the bow waves. They enjoy the company of others and often live in huge communities numbering hundreds, or even thousands, of individuals. But porpoises are very different. Shy and retiring creatures, they keep themselves to themselves and are usually quite difficult to see properly. They rarely jump out of the water, and most of them prefer to live alone or in small groups. They are generally smaller and chubbier than dolphins, ranging in size from the tiny Gulf of California porpoise, which measures as little as 1.3m (4ft 3in) in length, to the spectacled and Dall's porpoises which grow to 2.2m (7ft).

Living on the edge

Porpoises live dangerous lives. They are eaten by sharks and killer whales and many are hunted by fishermen for food. But one of the greatest threats they face is from fishing nets, which are a common - and deadly - hazard around many of the world's seas and coastlines. They are difficult to detect in the water, so the porpoises get tangled up in the mesh, and drown.

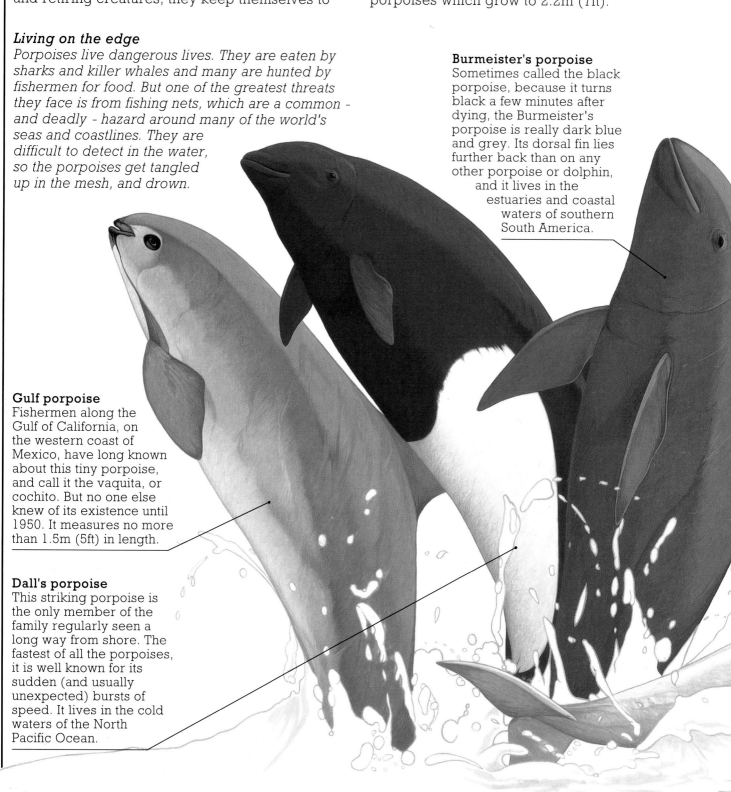

Burmeister's porpoise

Sometimes called the black porpoise, because it turns black a few minutes after dying, the Burmeister's porpoise is really dark blue and grey. Its dorsal fin lies further back than on any other porpoise or dolphin, and it lives in the estuaries and coastal waters of southern South America.

Gulf porpoise

Fishermen along the Gulf of California, on the western coast of Mexico, have long known about this tiny porpoise, and call it the vaquita, or cochito. But no one else knew of its existence until 1950. It measures no more than 1.5m (5ft) in length.

Dall's porpoise

This striking porpoise is the only member of the family regularly seen a long way from shore. The fastest of all the porpoises, it is well known for its sudden (and usually unexpected) bursts of speed. It lives in the cold waters of the North Pacific Ocean.

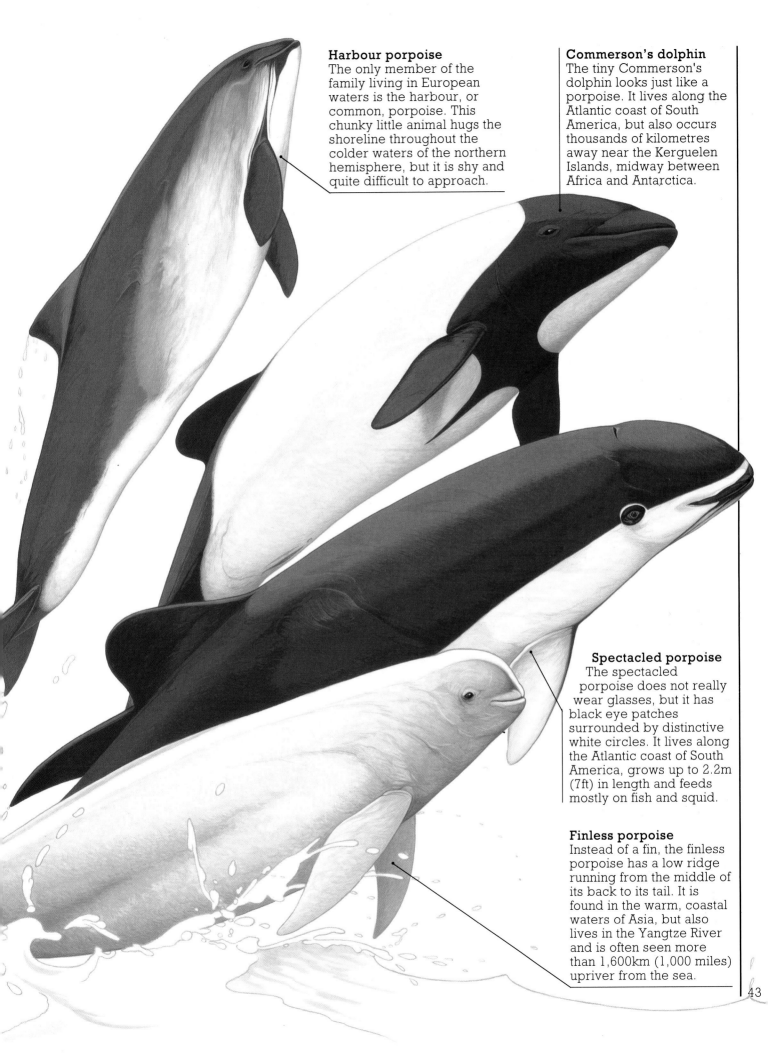

Harbour porpoise
The only member of the family living in European waters is the harbour, or common, porpoise. This chunky little animal hugs the shoreline throughout the colder waters of the northern hemisphere, but it is shy and quite difficult to approach.

Commerson's dolphin
The tiny Commerson's dolphin looks just like a porpoise. It lives along the Atlantic coast of South America, but also occurs thousands of kilometres away near the Kerguelen Islands, midway between Africa and Antarctica.

Spectacled porpoise
The spectacled porpoise does not really wear glasses, but it has black eye patches surrounded by distinctive white circles. It lives along the Atlantic coast of South America, grows up to 2.2m (7ft) in length and feeds mostly on fish and squid.

Finless porpoise
Instead of a fin, the finless porpoise has a low ridge running from the middle of its back to its tail. It is found in the warm, coastal waters of Asia, but also lives in the Yangtze River and is often seen more than 1,600km (1,000 miles) upriver from the sea.

RIVER LIFE

Most whales, dolphins and porpoises live in the sea. But there is a small and rather shy family, called the river dolphins, which prefers to live in freshwater. River dolphins inhabit some of the largest and muddiest rivers of Asia and South America. With one exception (the Franciscana), they never venture into the sea. They are peculiar animals, with very poor eyesight, huge numbers of pointed teeth, long slender beaks, small dorsal fins and a strange habit of swimming on their sides, or even upside-down. Despite their widely separated homes, which stretch from the Amazon river in Brazil, to the Yangtze river in China, they look alike and have adapted to their environment in similar ways. They are small animals, rarely more than 3m (10ft) long, and are difficult to see in the wild.

Suffering in silence
River dolphins are the forgotten members of the family. But they are in more serious trouble than many of their sea-going relatives. Their river homes are blocked by dams, and polluted by factories and towns that pour their waste straight into the water. They battle for space with boats, and are hunted for their oil and meat, or simply shot for "fun". They even get caught up in fishing gear and drown.

Black paradise fish

Yangtze river dolphin
The Yangtze river dolphin is one of the rarest animals in the world. Also known as the baiji, the Chinese river dolphin, or the whitefin dolphin, there are now fewer than 300 left, scattered along a 1,400km (875-mile) stretch of the Yangtze river, in China.

Ganges susu
Ganges river dolphins are often called "susus" because of the "susu" noise they make when they breathe out. Unlike most other river dolphins, they often leap right out of the water. This may be an alarm signal, warning other dolphins of danger.

Indus susu
In the muddy Indus river, in Pakistan, strange grey shapes can sometimes be seen swimming around in circles. They are Indus river dolphins, or susus, that seem to enjoy "looping the loop" underwater. They are rare animals with only about 500 surviviors left.

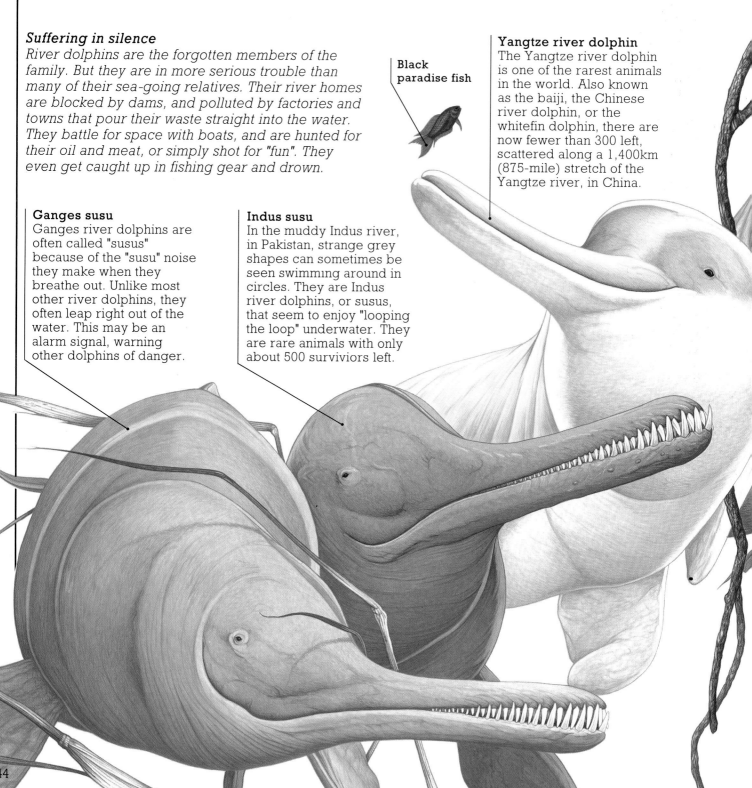

Amazon river dolphin

Also known as pink porpoises or boutus, these are the largest of the river dolphins. They are inquisitive creatures that live in the flooded forests of the Orinoco and Amazon river systems in South America, often swimming in small, tightly-packed groups.

Seeing with sound

River dolphins live in some of the muddiest rivers in the world, so they build up a "picture" of their surroundings with the help of sound. They make noises which bounce back from nearby objects and warn them if there is something in the murky water. This system is called "echolocation", and is similar to the system used by bats to find their way around in the dark.

The waves of sound bounce back

The waves of sound are sent out

Franciscana

The little Franciscana, or La Plata river dolphin, does not live in rivers. It is found along the Atlantic coast of South America and in estuaries, including the La Plata. Usually no more than 1.7m (5ft 6in) long, it is one of the smallest dolphins.

Tucuxi

The tucuxi is found in shallow waters all along the north-eastern coast of South America, and in the rivers of the Amazon Basin. It is not a real river dolphin, but is as happy in freshwater as it is in the sea. It shares part of its home with the Amazon river dolphin.

Common dolphin

The sea-going dolphins are quite different to their river relatives. The common dolphin, for example, rarely enters rivers. It has a short beak, and good eyesight, both above and below the surface. It often swims very fast and enjoys doing acrobatics and bow-riding (page 40). It lives in large schools that sometimes contain several thousand.

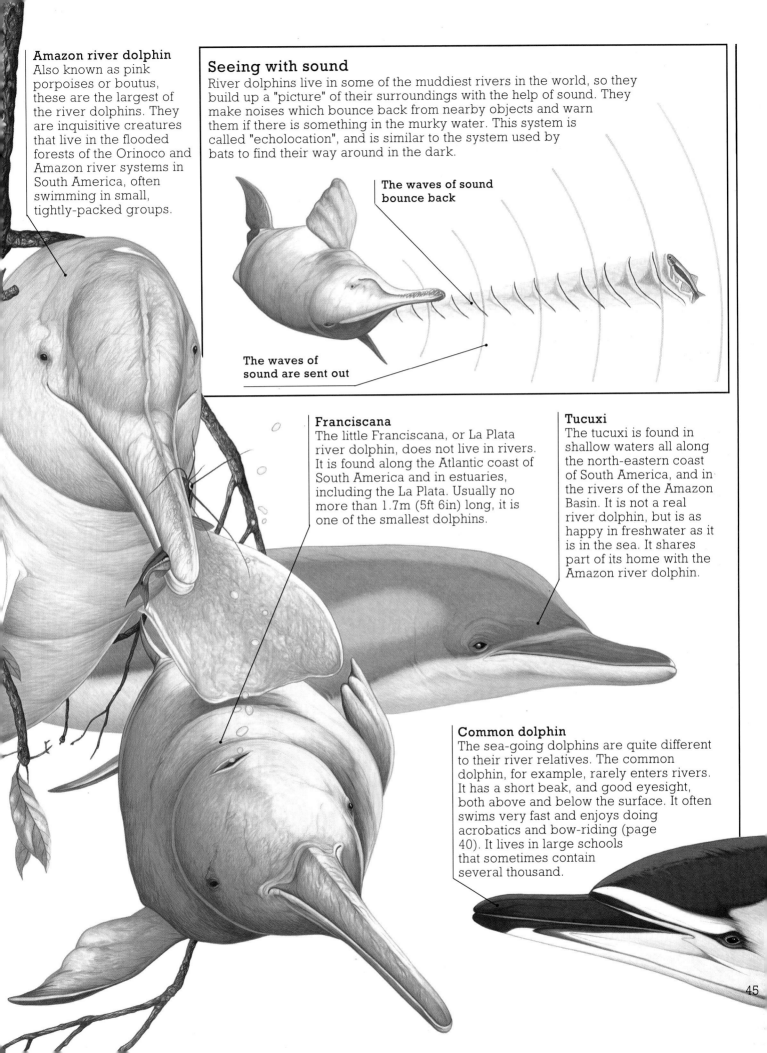

SOUNDS OF THE SEA

The sea is far from silent. It is full of the sounds of animals talking to one another underwater. Whales, dolphins and porpoises are real gossips and make a range of different squeaks, squawks, whistles, clicks, rattles and groans. Talking helps to keep them together when they are swimming as a group. It also means they can work together during the excitement of a hunt. But it can be much more specific than that - warning of danger, shouting for help, calling for a mate, threatening an enemy, suggesting a game or even discussing lunch.

Their sounds may have "personal signatures", helping them to identify one another by their calls, in the same way that we can recognize different people by their voices. Many species have also found ingenious ways of making spectacular sounds with their tails, flippers, jaws and other parts of their bodies, and these have their own special meanings.

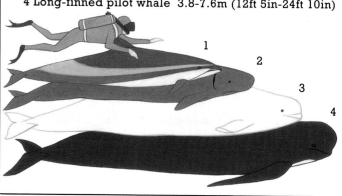

1 Fraser's dolphin 2.3-2.6m (7ft 6in-8ft 6in)
2 Pygmy sperm whale 2.7-3.4m (8ft 9in-11ft 2in)
3 Beluga whale 2.7-4.5m (8ft 9in-14ft 8in)
4 Long-finned pilot whale 3.8-7.6m (12ft 5in-24ft 10in)

No need to shout
Sound travels 4.5 times faster and much further underwater than it does in the air. So one animal can tell other members of its group where it is, who it is and what it is doing - even from a long distance away. Underwater communications across several kilometres of ocean are quite common.

Facial expressions
A beluga whale can smile, frown and may even appear to be blowing a kiss. It is not necessarily feeling happy, cross, or romantic, but each time it changes the expression on its face, it is sending an important signal to other members of the herd.

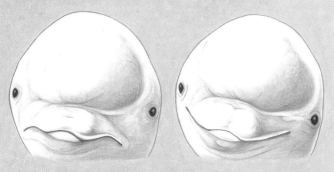

The beluga is unique among whales in being able to change the shape of its lips, so that it seems to us to be smiling happily or looking sad.

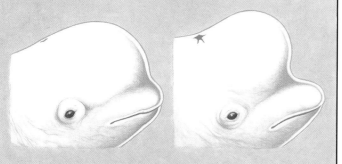

The beluga can even change the shape of its forehead. This extraordinary lump feels, to the touch, rather like a balloon filled with sand.

Jaw-clapping
When a long-finned pilot whale is annoyed, it snaps its jaws shut, producing a sharp explosive sound. This jaw-clapping acts as a warning to other whales to watch out, and is used mainly by older animals.

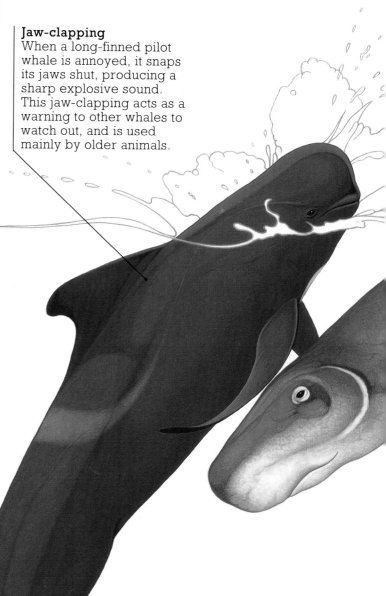

Swingin' humpbacks

Male humpback whales are the only animals which can boast a top-selling record in the pop charts. When their songs were first heard in the 1970s, many people were captivated by the melodious moans, groans, roars, snores, squeaks and whistles which form some of the longest and most complex songs in the animal kingdom. They sing throughout the day and night, with only brief one-minute pauses for breath. Most of the singing takes place at their breeding grounds (pages 26-27).

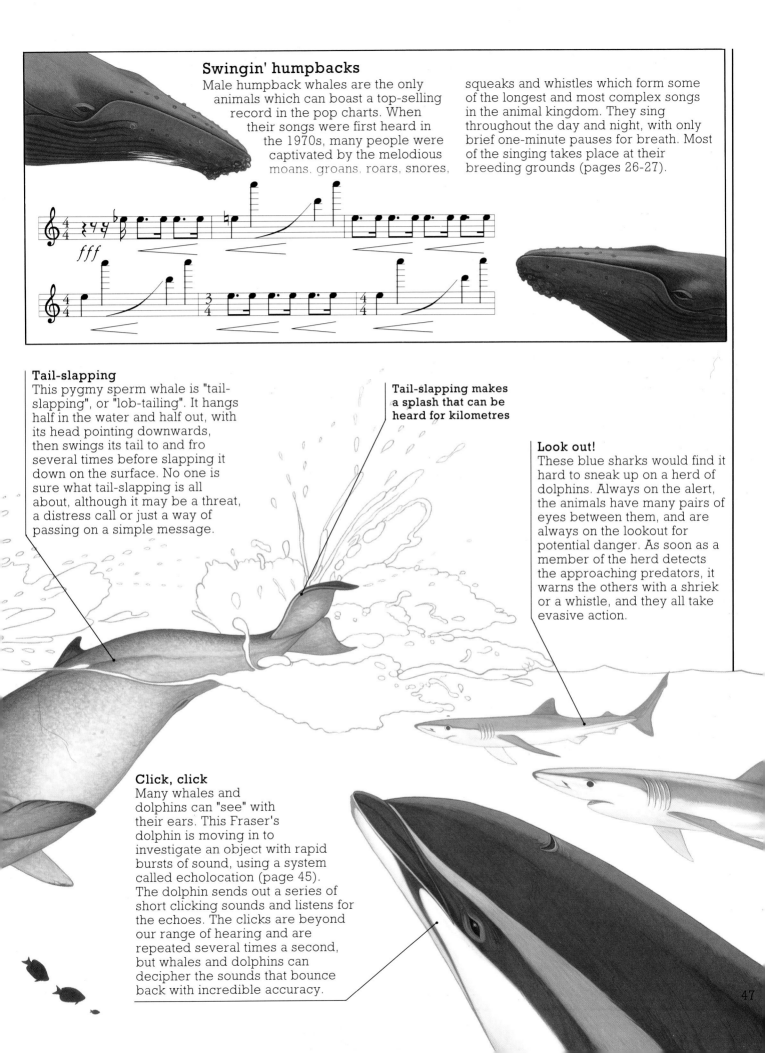

Tail-slapping

This pygmy sperm whale is "tail-slapping", or "lob-tailing". It hangs half in the water and half out, with its head pointing downwards, then swings its tail to and fro several times before slapping it down on the surface. No one is sure what tail-slapping is all about, although it may be a threat, a distress call or just a way of passing on a simple message.

Tail-slapping makes a splash that can be heard for kilometres

Look out!

These blue sharks would find it hard to sneak up on a herd of dolphins. Always on the alert, the animals have many pairs of eyes between them, and are always on the lookout for potential danger. As soon as a member of the herd detects the approaching predators, it warns the others with a shriek or a whistle, and they all take evasive action.

Click, click

Many whales and dolphins can "see" with their ears. This Fraser's dolphin is moving in to investigate an object with rapid bursts of sound, using a system called echolocation (page 45). The dolphin sends out a series of short clicking sounds and listens for the echoes. The clicks are beyond our range of hearing and are repeated several times a second, but whales and dolphins can decipher the sounds that bounce back with incredible accuracy.

BREACHING

Whales sometimes launch themselves into the air like torpedos. They jump right out of the water and then fall back in with a tremendous splash. This strange form of behaviour, known as "breaching", has puzzled scientists for many years. Most whales have been seen breaching at one time or another, and babies often begin to learn this spectacular "trick" when they are only a few weeks old. Even 150-tonne blue whales are able to breach. But there are four real experts - humpback, right, grey and sperm whales - that breach more often than all the others. They seem to find it "infectious" and, when one animal starts breaching, its neighbours cannot resist joining in. Sometimes, they never seem to want to stop. One humpback whale was seen breaching 130 times in 75 minutes.

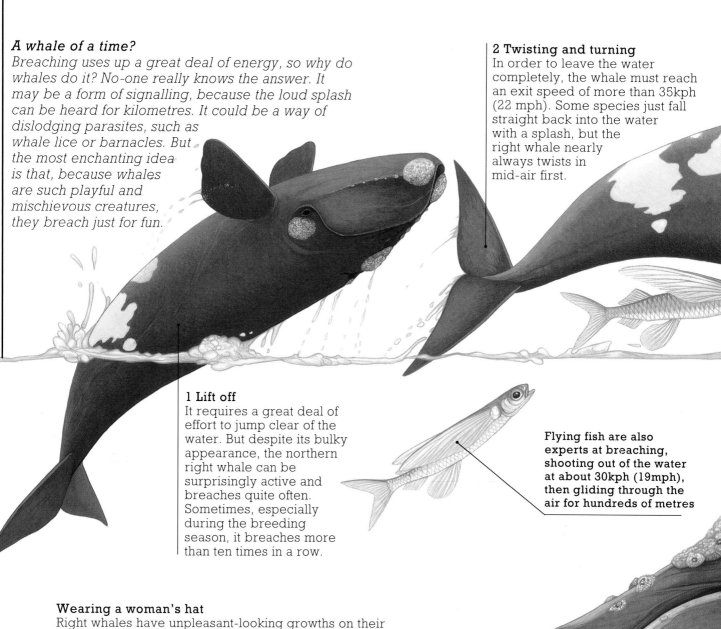

A whale of a time?
Breaching uses up a great deal of energy, so why do whales do it? No-one really knows the answer. It may be a form of signalling, because the loud splash can be heard for kilometres. It could be a way of dislodging parasites, such as whale lice or barnacles. But the most enchanting idea is that, because whales are such playful and mischievous creatures, they breach just for fun.

2 Twisting and turning
In order to leave the water completely, the whale must reach an exit speed of more than 35kph (22 mph). Some species just fall straight back into the water with a splash, but the right whale nearly always twists in mid-air first.

1 Lift off
It requires a great deal of effort to jump clear of the water. But despite its bulky appearance, the northern right whale can be surprisingly active and breaches quite often. Sometimes, especially during the breeding season, it breaches more than ten times in a row.

Flying fish are also experts at breaching, shooting out of the water at about 30kph (19mph), then gliding through the air for hundreds of metres

Wearing a woman's hat
Right whales have unpleasant-looking growths on their skin. These are called "callosities", and first appear when the animals are very young. They are usually infested with colourful colonies of barnacles, whale lice and parasitic worms. Most of them occur on the chin, on the sides of the head, above the eyes, on the lower lips, and near the blowholes. But one of the largest is on the top of the head and is called the "bonnet", because it looks like a woman's hat.

Leaps and bounds

Killer whales often leap out of the water, and genuinely seem to enjoy landing on their backs, sides or stomachs with a noisy splash. Cuvier's beaked whales also leap out of the water, but at a much steeper angle. Minke whales are not enthusiastic acrobats, but when they breach, they do it with style - sometimes doing a complete arc in the air and diving back in head-first with hardly a splash.

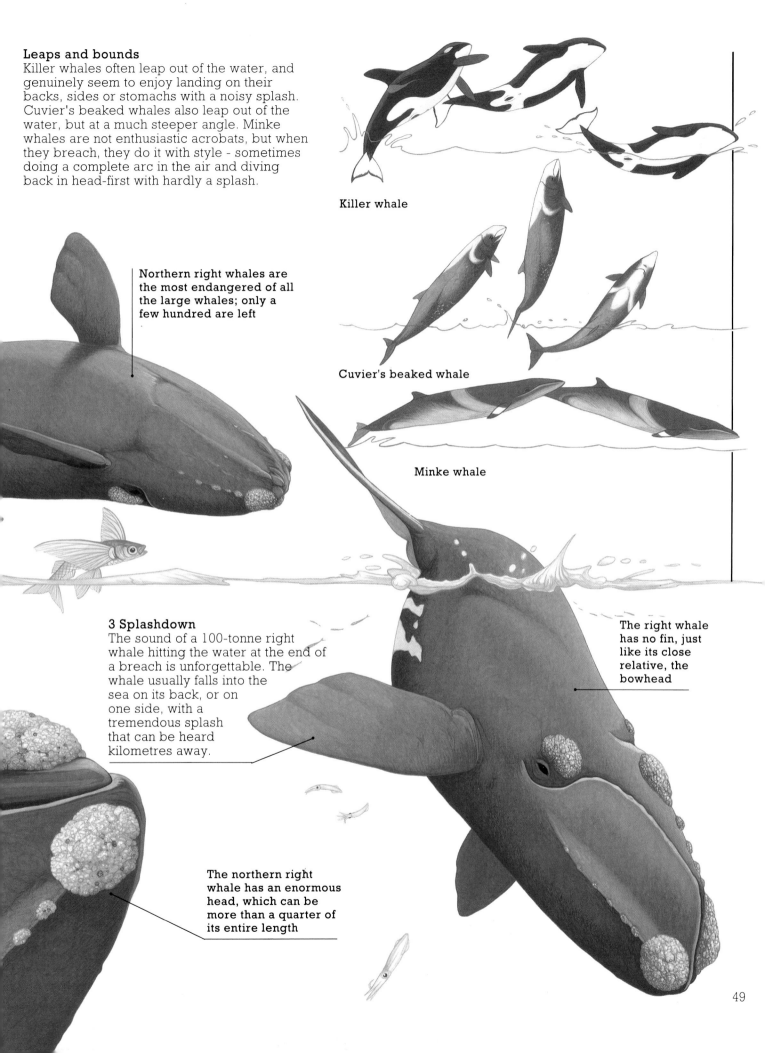

Killer whale

Cuvier's beaked whale

Minke whale

Northern right whales are the most endangered of all the large whales; only a few hundred are left

3 Splashdown
The sound of a 100-tonne right whale hitting the water at the end of a breach is unforgettable. The whale usually falls into the sea on its back, or on one side, with a tremendous splash that can be heard kilometres away.

The right whale has no fin, just like its close relative, the bowhead

The northern right whale has an enormous head, which can be more than a quarter of its entire length

49

RECORD BREAKERS

Whales, dolphins and porpoises come in all shapes and sizes. They belong to the same group, and they all live in water, yet they have adapted to their environment in many different ways. Some of them are long and thin, others are short and fat. Some have huge fins, others have no fins at all. There are those with long, pointed flippers, and others with small, paddle-shaped flippers. Some are bright and conspicuous, others are drab and difficult to see. Some are noisy and bold, while others are shy and retiring. Indeed, there is so much variety that it is often difficult to believe that animals as diverse as the harbour porpoise and the humpback whale, for example, really do belong to the same group. So it is not surprising that, between them, the cetaceans break a number of world records. The most famous is the blue whale, which is the biggest animal ever to have lived on earth.

Choosing a winner
Selecting record-breaking whales, dolphins and porpoises can be very difficult, because no two individuals are exactly alike. Even within the same species, they can vary from one animal to the next. These are some of the more unmistakable record-breakers. They do not all hold world records, but they are outstanding members of the family.

Largest
The blue whale is the largest animal ever to have lived on earth. The all-time record-holder was a female found in the Antarctic - at an incredible 33.58m (110ft) long. The heaviest ever recorded was another female. She weighed in at 190 tonnes, which is equivalent to more than 2,500 people. Blue whales in the southern hemisphere tend to be the largest, and females are larger than males.

Despite its enormous size, the blue whale is surprisingly slim and streamlined

Baby blue whales drink 380 litres (84 gallons) of their mothers' rich milk every day

Largest baby
When they are first born, baby blue whales are 7m (23ft) long, and weigh more than two tonnes. Every day, they gain 90kg (198lb) - more than the weight of a fully-grown man. By the time they are weaned, the whales have more than doubled in length and weigh an incredible 20 tonnes.

The flippers of humpback whales are covered in strange lumps and bumps

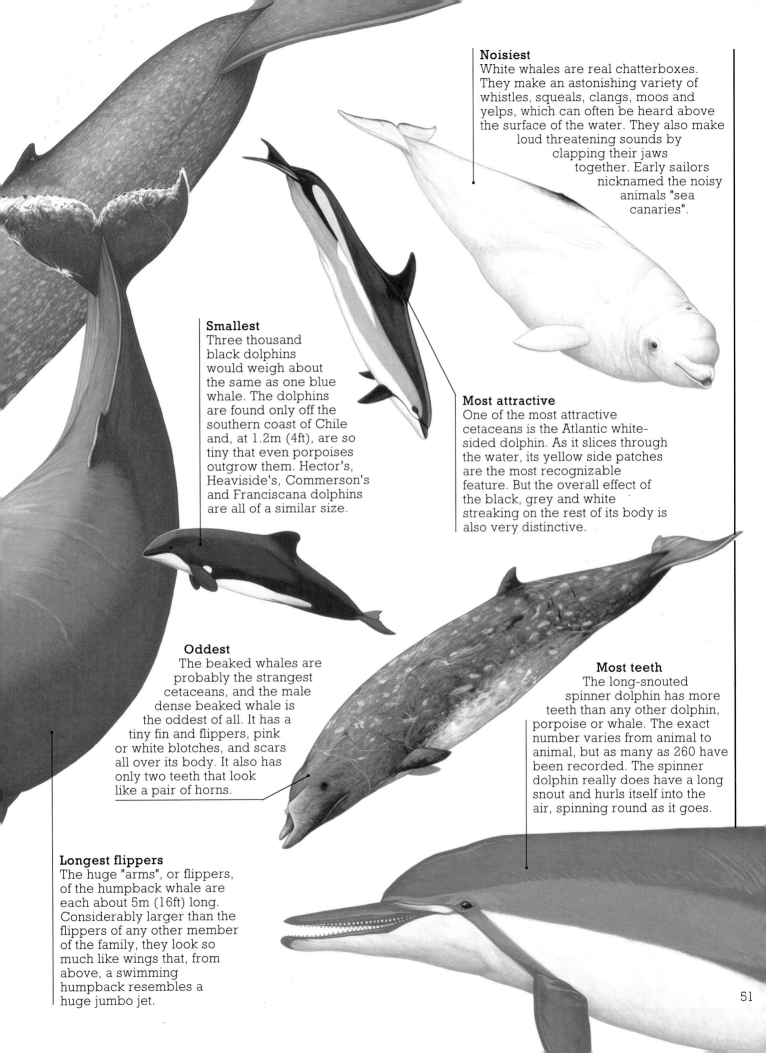

Noisiest
White whales are real chatterboxes. They make an astonishing variety of whistles, squeals, clangs, moos and yelps, which can often be heard above the surface of the water. They also make loud threatening sounds by clapping their jaws together. Early sailors nicknamed the noisy animals "sea canaries".

Smallest
Three thousand black dolphins would weigh about the same as one blue whale. The dolphins are found only off the southern coast of Chile and, at 1.2m (4ft), are so tiny that even porpoises outgrow them. Hector's, Heaviside's, Commerson's and Franciscana dolphins are all of a similar size.

Most attractive
One of the most attractive cetaceans is the Atlantic white-sided dolphin. As it slices through the water, its yellow side patches are the most recognizable feature. But the overall effect of the black, grey and white streaking on the rest of its body is also very distinctive.

Oddest
The beaked whales are probably the strangest cetaceans, and the male dense beaked whale is the oddest of all. It has a tiny fin and flippers, pink or white blotches, and scars all over its body. It also has only two teeth that look like a pair of horns.

Most teeth
The long-snouted spinner dolphin has more teeth than any other dolphin, porpoise or whale. The exact number varies from animal to animal, but as many as 260 have been recorded. The spinner dolphin really does have a long snout and hurls itself into the air, spinning round as it goes.

Longest flippers
The huge "arms", or flippers, of the humpback whale are each about 5m (16ft) long. Considerably larger than the flippers of any other member of the family, they look so much like wings that, from above, a swimming humpback resembles a huge jumbo jet.

HIGH SPEED CHASE

The world's seas and oceans are full of superb swimmers. Sealions, otters, sharks, sailfish, penguins and thousands of others could easily beat human swimmers if they were challenged to a race. Some of them can accelerate to such phenomenal speeds that many boats would find it hard to keep up. But it is much more difficult to move through water than air, so these creatures have had to develop special techniques to be able to swim so fast. Otters kick with their hind legs, doing a kind of doggy-paddle. Sealions swim with their foreflippers, "flying" along underwater like penguins. But the fastest of them all use their tails, like powerful engines, to propel them through the water. Sharks and other fish swing their tails from side to side, while whales, dolphins and porpoises beat theirs up and down. It can take a long time to accelerate, but the power of the tails is enormous.

King penguin
Penguins cannot fly in the air but they use their wings, which are modified into flippers, to "fly" underwater. Their feet act as rudders to steer to the left or right. They use the same "porpoising" technique as many dolphins and porpoises, plunging in and out of the sea at speeds of up to 15kph (9mph) or more.

You can sometimes hear a porpoising penguin gasp for breath each time it breaks the surface

Fin whale
Large whales normally swim quite slowly, and rarely seem to be in a hurry. But they can move incredibly quickly when danger threatens or if they are frightened. One of the fastest of them all is the fin whale, which can reach speeds of over 37kph (23mph).

Striped dolphin
Striped dolphins enjoy swimming fast and are able to reach speeds of up to 30kph (19mph). As they slice through the water with effortless ease, only two thirds of the dolphins in a school may be underwater at one time. The others are leaping high into the air.

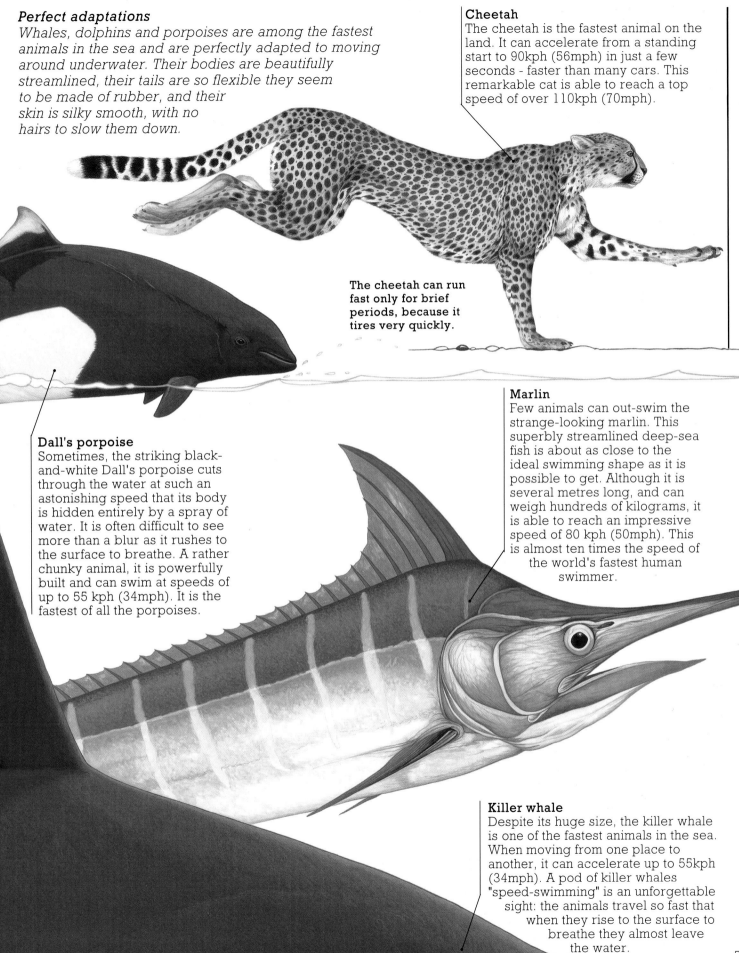

Perfect adaptations
Whales, dolphins and porpoises are among the fastest animals in the sea and are perfectly adapted to moving around underwater. Their bodies are beautifully streamlined, their tails are so flexible they seem to be made of rubber, and their skin is silky smooth, with no hairs to slow them down.

Cheetah
The cheetah is the fastest animal on the land. It can accelerate from a standing start to 90kph (56mph) in just a few seconds - faster than many cars. This remarkable cat is able to reach a top speed of over 110kph (70mph).

The cheetah can run fast only for brief periods, because it tires very quickly.

Marlin
Few animals can out-swim the strange-looking marlin. This superbly streamlined deep-sea fish is about as close to the ideal swimming shape as it is possible to get. Although it is several metres long, and can weigh hundreds of kilograms, it is able to reach an impressive speed of 80 kph (50mph). This is almost ten times the speed of the world's fastest human swimmer.

Dall's porpoise
Sometimes, the striking black-and-white Dall's porpoise cuts through the water at such an astonishing speed that its body is hidden entirely by a spray of water. It is often difficult to see more than a blur as it rushes to the surface to breathe. A rather chunky animal, it is powerfully built and can swim at speeds of up to 55 kph (34mph). It is the fastest of all the porpoises.

Killer whale
Despite its huge size, the killer whale is one of the fastest animals in the sea. When moving from one place to another, it can accelerate up to 55kph (34mph). A pod of killer whales "speed-swimming" is an unforgettable sight: the animals travel so fast that when they rise to the surface to breathe they almost leave the water.

RESCUE

Every year, thousands of whales, dolphins and porpoises are found stranded, alive or dead, on beaches all over the world. They may be alone or in groups, young or old, male or female, large or small, and healthy or unwell. But why does this happen? It is one of the great mysteries of the animal kingdom, and we still do not have an answer. Some strandings are easy to explain: the animals simply die at sea and are washed ashore with the tides and currents. But no one can account for the live animals that become stranded. They may be trying to escape from predators; they may be ill and need somewhere to rest, where they can keep themselves above the water to breathe. They may have panicked because of an earthquake or electrical storm; or they may simply be lost.

Magnetic maps
Whales and dolphins have an extra sense called "biomagnetism". This enables them to detect variations in the earth's magnetic field which they may use, like a map, to find their way around. But the magnetic field is always changing, so sometimes the whales may not be where they think they are. If they follow the wrong route, it could lead them towards the shore, and almost certain death.

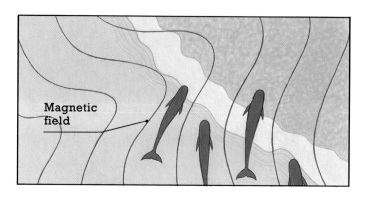

Magnetic field

Pilot whales
Some whales are more easily stranded than others - and pilot whales seem to suffer more than most. The social bonds between them are so strong that they are reluctant to desert one another. Whatever happens to one animal affects the entire group.

Helpless
Pilot whales are a strange shape and, as the tide goes out, they topple over onto one side. When the tide comes back in, they usually drown because the water covers their blowholes long before they can right themselves.

Rescue - stage one
The first thing to do when you find stranded whales is to get expert help. While waiting for this to arrive, it is possible to make them a little more comfortable. Make sure they can breathe, and nothing is blocking their blowholes.

Cooperating

In October 1988, three grey whales, trapped in a small clearing in the Arctic ice, became internationally famous overnight. A massive rescue attempt was launched to help them. One of the whales died, but the other two were saved in an operation involving Russian ice-breakers, American scientists and local people. The rescue cost an estimated $1 million.

The three whales used the clearing in the ice as a breathing-hole

Stranded whales used to be an important source of food and fuel for many coastal people - and they were delivered right to their doorsteps!

Against their will

Helping beached whales can be an upsetting experience. Every time they are pushed or pulled into deeper water, they try to swim back to shore and beach themselves again. So returning beached whales to the sea can require many people, as well as boats, cranes and ropes.

Follow the leader

Pilot whales will not swim to freedom unless their group leaders are safe and well, even though this may mean that they are risking their own lives. Sometimes it is necessary to hold the leaders a long way offshore before the others can be lured away from the beach to join them.

Rescue - stage two

Shade the whales from the burning rays of the sun and keep their skin wet. Take great care not to let incoming water enter their blowholes. Above all, do not frighten the animals by crowding round them - and never tug on their flippers or flukes.

BEAKED WHALES

Beaked whales are the strangest and most elusive cetaceans. We know very little about them, because they live far from land and avoid ships and boats. So far, 19 species have been identified, although there could be others lurking in the ocean depths, waiting to be discovered. Most of the information we have about them has been gleaned from dead animals washed ashore and, indeed, some species have never been seen alive.

Beaked whales are medium-sized whales and, as their name suggests, have unmistakeable crocodile-like beaks. Most of the males have only two teeth, and these grow into weird tusks that peer out of their mouths at the front or sides. The teeth of the females are invisible, because they remain inside their gums.

It's all in a name

Baird, Shepherd, Hubb and Gray are just some of the scientists who have given their names to beaked whales. Most members of this mysterious family have been named after the people who discovered or described them. However, other scientists sometimes give them alternative names, which makes it all very confusing.

New whale found!

One day in 1976, an American zoologist bought a strange skull from a stall in a fish market in Peru. On his return home, he made an exciting discovery - the skull belonged to a new species of beaked whale. It is the smallest of all the known beaked whales, measuring only 3.7m (12ft) long.

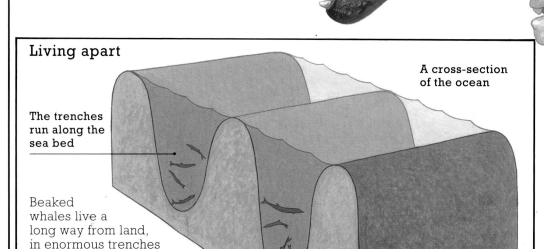

Living apart

A cross-section of the ocean

The trenches run along the sea bed

Beaked whales live a long way from land, in enormous trenches in the deep, open ocean. These may have kept populations apart so that, over millions of years, the animals evolved separately. But the conditions in the trenches were probably similar and so the whales are very similar in appearance.

The bones of the matter

This is the skull of a dense beaked whale. The male usually has only two teeth. It is easy to see why the owner of this skull looks so strange, with those two teeth growing high into the air from the weird bulges on its jawbone.

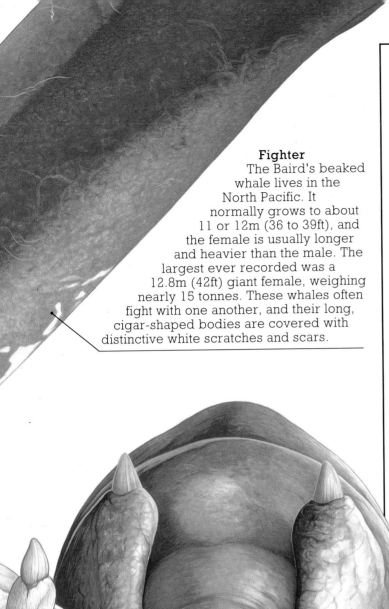

Fighter
The Baird's beaked whale lives in the North Pacific. It normally grows to about 11 or 12m (36 to 39ft), and the female is usually longer and heavier than the male. The largest ever recorded was a 12.8m (42ft) giant female, weighing nearly 15 tonnes. These whales often fight with one another, and their long, cigar-shaped bodies are covered with distinctive white scratches and scars.

Teeth or horns?
The dense-beaked whale is one of the oddest-looking animals in the world. Its two teeth grow upwards like a massive pair of horns. Sometimes, they are encrusted with barnacles and, when the whale swims near the surface, they look like two small bushes riding along on the waves.

Spot the difference
Beaked whales are very difficult to tell apart. It is almost impossible to see the difference between females or young whales, although many of the males can be identified by the shape and position of their tusk-like teeth.

The rare Shepherd's beaked whale has up to 116 teeth, and the male also has a pair of tusks

The southern bottlenose whale has either two or four large conical teeth sticking out at the front

The strap-toothed beaked whale has two teeth which curve around its upper jaw

The True's beaked whale has two tiny teeth which are at the front of its mouth

The Hubb's beaked whale has triangular teeth, and seems to be wearing a white "cap"

The gingko-toothed beaked whale's teeth look like the fan-shaped leaves of the gingko tree

The Scamperdown beaked whale has two small teeth at the sides of its slender beak

The Stejneger's beaked whale has two huge, and very distinctive, flame-shaped teeth

SAVE THE WHALE!

A few centuries ago, the sea was full of whales, dolphins and porpoises. Fishermen and sailors used to see them spouting and breaching all the time. But the sea is a much duller place today, because whales and their relatives have all but disappeared from many parts of the world. The great whales were hunted almost to the point of extinction and, although all commercial whaling is now officially banned, small numbers of them are still being killed. More than 100,000 dolphins and porpoises are slaughtered every year for their meat, and many more drown in fishing nets. Pollution is yet another major threat, as we dump our rubbish and waste into the sea. Despite these and many other dangers, no member of the whale family has become extinct in modern times. But some species are in serious trouble and, unless they are protected, we may lose them altogether.

No safety in numbers
At the turn of the century, there were 250,000 blue whales around Antarctica but, after years of intensive whaling, there are now fewer than 700 left. If this pattern is not to be repeated, we must take better care of the whales and dolphins alive today.

Whaling
In 1864, a single event dramatically changed all whaling operations. Svend Foyn, a Norwegian, developed a terrible harpoon which, instead of being hand-held, could be fired from a cannon. Two or three seconds after it hits a whale, a grenade at the end of the harpoon explodes inside the animal's body. The whales did not stand a chance and, one by one, they were hunted almost to the point of extinction.

Explosive harpoons are still used today, on board the rusty Japanese whaling vessels that patrol the Antarctic

Spinner dolphin

Tuna

In captivity

Bottlenose dolphins, spotted dolphins, pilot whales, killer whales, false killer whales and belugas are some of the species that perform tricks in marine parks and zoos all over the world. Most of the animals have been captured in the wild, and this upsets many people. They believe that whales and dolphins are unhappy in their artificial tanks, and say that it is cruel and insulting to make them perform tricks in front of an audience.

An unfair advantage

One particularly nasty method of tuna fishing involves underwater explosives. Helicopters are launched from huge boats to search for tuna and dolphins. When they find a school, they drop bombs to stun the animals ready for netting.

Commercial uses

Whales were originally hunted for their meat. But over the years their blubber, skin, teeth, bones and other parts of their bodies have been used to make many different products. Some of the goods, which also included bootlaces, shampoos, glue, polishes and drumskins, are shown here. Today, there are acceptable substitutes for all these products - so there is no need for the whales to be killed.

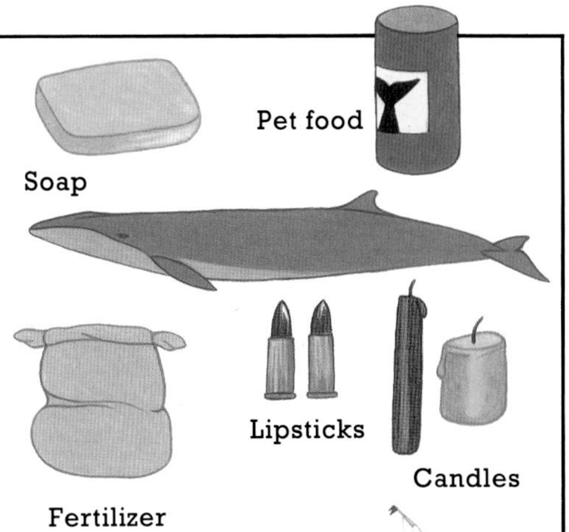

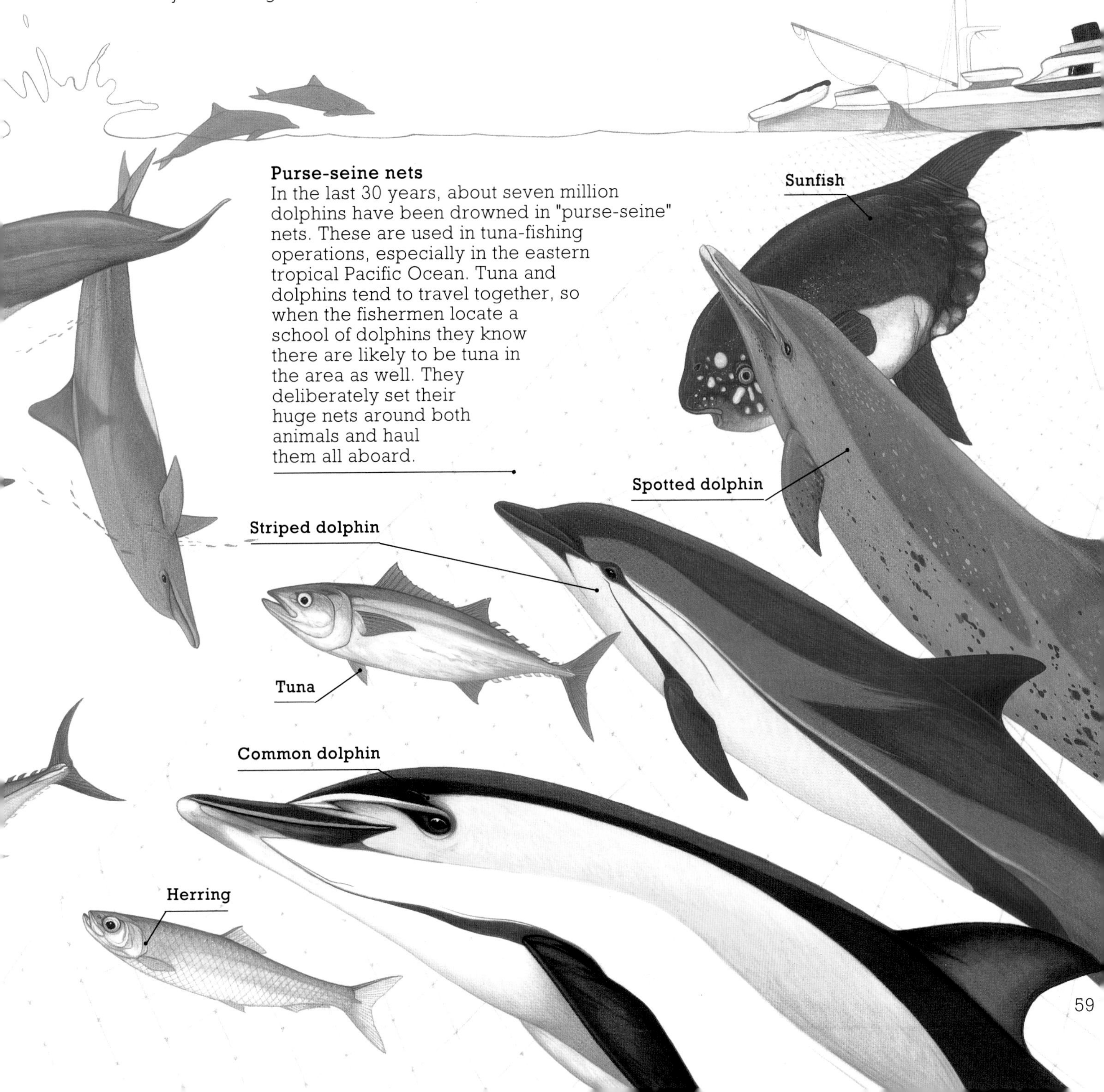

Soap

Pet food

Lipsticks

Candles

Fertilizer

Purse-seine nets

In the last 30 years, about seven million dolphins have been drowned in "purse-seine" nets. These are used in tuna-fishing operations, especially in the eastern tropical Pacific Ocean. Tuna and dolphins tend to travel together, so when the fishermen locate a school of dolphins they know there are likely to be tuna in the area as well. They deliberately set their huge nets around both animals and haul them all aboard.

Sunfish

Spotted dolphin

Striped dolphin

Tuna

Common dolphin

Herring

At risk

Some members of the whale family are in danger of becoming extinct. One of the rarest is the Yangtze river dolphin, with only 200-300 individuals left. There are also only a few hundred northern right whales surviving. But even common species are at risk, unless we can tackle the many threats they have to face almost every day of their lives.

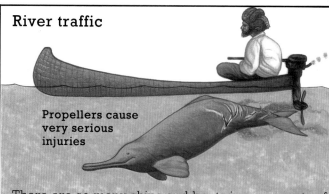

River traffic

Propellers cause very serious injuries

There are so many ships and boats in some parts of the world that whales and dolphins can be badly injured by them. Some of the river dolphins have a particularly difficult time dodging all the boat traffic in the busy waterways where they live.

Dumping oil

Several million tonnes of oil are released into the seas and oceans every year, and oil slicks have become a common sight in many parts of the world. No one knows the effect that oil has on whales and dolphins, but it certainly damages their underwater world.

Walls of death

Fishermen in some parts of the world use enormous nets called "driftnets". These can be up to 50km (31 miles) long and hang in the water like curtains, to a depth of more than 10m (33ft). They are virtually invisible and, as they drift around in the sea, catch spotted, striped, common and spinner dolphins, as well as whales, turtles, seabirds and other marine animals.

Long-fin tuna

Pilchard

More than 5,000 dolphins and porpoises like this Burmeister's porpoise, are killed by Chilean fishermen every year for crab bait

Chilean fishermen call dolphins and porpoises "tontitas", or "silly ones", because they are so friendly and easy to kill

Pollution

Pollution is everywhere - in the air, on land, in freshwater and in the sea. Industrial wastes, oil, untreated sewage and pesticides pour into the sea in huge quantities, and harm whales and their relatives. Even household rubbish can be harmful - dolphins' beaks get tangled in plastic.

Crab bait

In Chile, dolphins and porpoises are used as bait to catch southern king crabs in pots. Many thousand Commerson's dolphins, Burmeister's porpoises and black dolphins, as well as fur seals, sealions, penguins and other wildlife, are killed every year for this purpose.

Towards a better future

Whales, dolphins and porpoises have been hunted for hundreds of years, but today our attitude towards them is gradually changing. After many years of campaigning by conservation groups, most countries have at last banned the killing. The animals still face many threats, of course, but their future is not as bleak as it was only a few years ago.

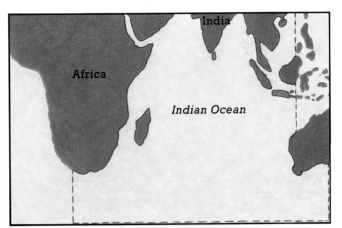

Safe waters

In 1979, the entire Indian Ocean was declared a sanctuary for whales, dolphins and porpoises. It is a huge area, and the only sanctuary of its kind in the world - somewhere safe where the animals can live without being hunted commercially.

Against the odds

The people in this inflatable dinghy are risking their own lives to save a whale from the hunters. They are weaving backwards and forwards between the whaling vessel and its quarry, to prevent the frightened animal from being shot with an explosive harpoon.

Whale watching

For many people, watching whales and dolphins in the wild is an experience of a lifetime. As well as being fun, it encourages an active interest in their well-being, and proves that the animals are worth more alive than dead.

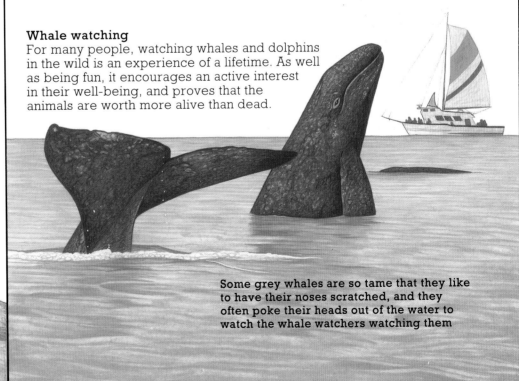

Some grey whales are so tame that they like to have their noses scratched, and they often poke their heads out of the water to watch the whale watchers watching them

STORY OF A WHALE

Hughie the humpback whale was born in 1961 which, by whale standards, makes him an old man. He was about 5m (16ft 5in) long at birth and has since grown to a strapping 13m (42ft 7in) adult, with many wives and umpteen children. If he is lucky, he may live until the turn of the century but, at the grand old age of 40, he will find it hard to defend himself against marauding killer whales, and to migrate between his breeding grounds in the Caribbean and his feeding grounds in Canada. Like many humpback whales, he has had an eventful life and some extraordinary experiences over the years. He is widely travelled and, on one occasion, nearly drowned in a fisherman's net. He has been studied by scientists since he was a teenager and has even been photographed by boatloads of excited tourists.

Hughie the humpback

This story is based on actual sightings and events, recorded by dozens of scientists over many years. Although Hughie himself is an imaginary animal, there are many humpback whales just like him, living out eventful lives in many parts of the world.

Killer whale attack

When he was a teenager, Hughie was attacked by a pod of killer whales. They harassed him for several minutes, and tried to bite chunks out of his flippers and fin. But he fought back with powerful swipes of his tail and managed to scare them away. He still has some of the scars from his frightening encounter.

LABRADOR

Hughie sometimes visits Labrador during the summer

Weekends away

Hughie spends every summer swimming around Newfoundland, in Canada. He joins other humpbacks to feed in the rich waters just off the coast. His mother showed him where to fish when he was less than a year old, and he has been returning to the same areas ever since. Sometimes, when food is in short supply, he takes a few days off and swims up to Labrador - but most of the time he is too busy fattening up for the winter to swim very far.

NEWFOUNDLAND

Hughie travels all around the coast of Newfoundland

In the autumn, Hughie migrates south towards his birthplace off Puerto Rico in the Caribbean, sometimes stopping on the way for a well-earned rest in Bermuda

Capelin beach

There is a long, sandy beach called St Vincent's, in eastern Newfoundland, which is famous for the humpback whales that visit it. In the summer months of June and July, hundreds of thousands of capelin swim onto the sand to lay their eggs. The huge shoals of these small fish attract Hughie and his friends to the beach every year. In their efforts to catch the capelin, the whales sometimes get so excited that they storm up the beach and have to push themselves back into the sea with their flippers.

Help!

Hughie once got tangled up in a fisherman's net near the coast in Newfoundland. The more he struggled the more entangled he became. Fortunately, within a few hours, he was spotted and a whale rescue team arrived to cut him free. After a brief pause to catch his breath, Hughie was able to swim away.

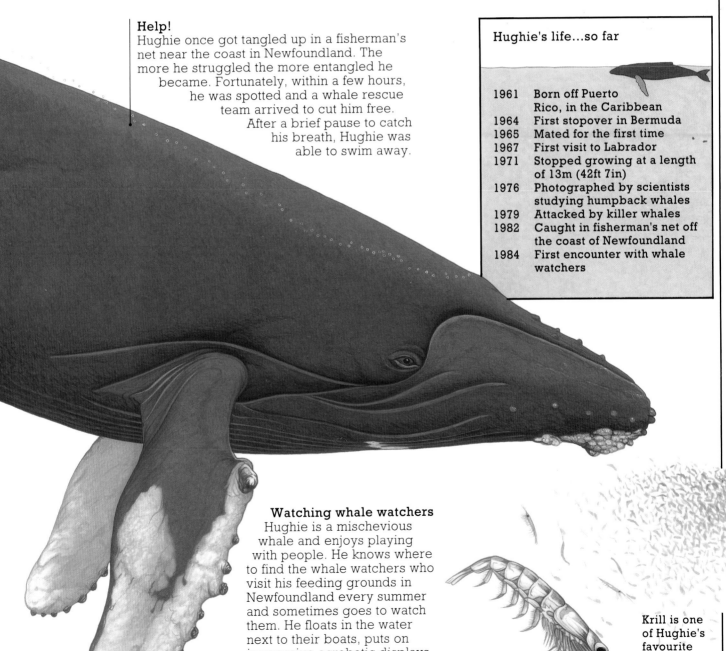

Hughie's life...so far

1961	Born off Puerto Rico, in the Caribbean
1964	First stopover in Bermuda
1965	Mated for the first time
1967	First visit to Labrador
1971	Stopped growing at a length of 13m (42ft 7in)
1976	Photographed by scientists studying humpback whales
1979	Attacked by killer whales
1982	Caught in fisherman's net off the coast of Newfoundland
1984	First encounter with whale watchers

Watching whale watchers

Hughie is a mischevious whale and enjoys playing with people. He knows where to find the whale watchers who visit his feeding grounds in Newfoundland every summer and sometimes goes to watch them. He floats in the water next to their boats, puts on impressive acrobatic displays and sometimes splashes them with his enormous tail.

Krill is one of Hughie's favourite foods

INDEX

Acknowledgements
Dorling Kindersley would like to thank Janet Abbott and Lynn Bresler for their help in producing this book..